Frommer's®

D0449918

New Orleans
day BY day
4th Edition

by Diana K. Schwam

Contents

Published by:

FrommerMedia LLC

Copyright © 2017 Frommer Media LLC, New York, NY. All rights reserved. No part of this publication may be reproduced, stored in a retrieval system or transmitted in any form or by any means, electronic, mechanical, photocopying, recording, scanning or otherwise, except as permitted under Sections 107 or 108 of the 1976 United States Copyright Act, without the prior written permission of the Publisher. Requests to the Publisher for permission should be addressed to http://www.frommers.com/support.

Frommer's is a trademark or registered trademark of Arthur Frommer.

ISBN: 978-1-62887-320-7 (print); 978-1-62887-321-4 (ebk)

Editorial Director: Pauline Frommer
Editor: Michael Kelly
Production Editors: Lindsay Conner, Kelly Henthorne
Photo Editor: Meghan Lamb
Cartographer: Liz Puhl

Front cover photos, left to right: Mardi Gras © Dustie / Shutterstock.com; Jackson Square buildings and Cathedral © photosounds / Shutterstock.com; Shrimp at Commander's Palace, Courtesy of Commander's Palace
Back cover photo: Mule-drawn carriage © pisaphotography / Shutterstock.com

For information on our other products and services, please go to Frommers.com/contactus.
Frommer's also publishes its books in a variety of electronic formats. Some content that appears in print may not be available in electronic formats.

Manufactured in China

5 4 3 2 1

About This Guide

Organizing your time. That's what this guide is all about.

Other guides give you long lists of things to see and do and then expect you to fit the pieces together. The Day by Day guides are different. These guides tell you the best of everything, and then they show you how to see it in the smartest, most time-efficient way. Our authors have designed detailed itineraries organized by time, neighborhood, or special interest. And each tour comes with a bulleted map that takes you from stop to stop.

Hoping to soak in the history of the French Quarter, visit some underwater friends at the Aquarium of the Americas, or see where some of the U.S.'s most famous writers spent their time and spun their tales? Planning a walk through the Garden District, or dinner and drinks where you can dance the night away to a local jazz or brass band? Whatever your interest or schedule, the Day by Days give you the smartest routes to follow. Not only do we take you to the top attractions, hotels, and restaurants, but we also help you access those special moments that locals get to experience—those "finds" that turn tourists into travelers.

The Day by Days are also your top choice if you're looking for one complete guide for all your travel needs. The best hotels and restaurants for every budget, the greatest shopping values, the wildest nightlife—it's all here.

Why should you trust our judgment? Because our authors personally visit each place they write about. They're an independent lot who say what they think and would never include places they wouldn't recommend to their best friends. They're also open to suggestions from readers. If you'd like to contact them, please send your comments our way at feedback@frommers.com, and we'll pass them on.

Enjoy your Day by Day guide—the most helpful travel companion you can buy. And have the trip of a lifetime.

About the Author

Diana K. Schwam, writer and strategic marketing consultant, has authored seven books, numerous articles, and scads of content about New Orleans. She followed a familiar path to the city: vacation, enrapture, return, return, return, fleur de lis tolerance, home ownership, tolerance of everything else, weight gain, contentment. In her spare time, she enjoys music, film, tennis, reading, biking, a well-balanced cocktail, and continued breathing. Ms. Schwam claps on the twos and fours. Usually.

An Additional Note

Please be advised that travel information is subject to change at any time—and this is especially true of prices. We therefore suggest that you write or call ahead for confirmation when making your travel plans. The authors, editors, and publisher cannot be held responsible for the experiences of readers while traveling. Your safety is important to us, however, so we encourage you to stay alert and be aware of your surroundings.

Star Ratings, Icons & Abbreviations

Every hotel, restaurant, and attraction listing in this guide has been ranked for quality, value, service, amenities, and special features using a **star-rating system**. Hotels, restaurants, attractions, shopping, and nightlife are rated on a scale of zero stars (recommended) to three stars (exceptional). In addition to the star-rating system, we also use a **kids** icon to point out the best bets for families. Within each tour, we recommend cafes, bars, or restaurants where you can take a break. Each of these stops appears in a shaded box marked with a coffee-cup-shaped bullet ☕.

The following **abbreviations** are used for credit cards:

AE	American Express	DISC	Discover	V	Visa
DC	Diners Club	MC	MasterCard		

Frommers.com

Frommer's travel resources don't end with this guide. Frommer's website, www.frommers.com, has travel information on more than 4,000 destinations. We update features regularly, giving you access to the most current trip-planning information and the best airfare, lodging, and car-rental bargains. You can also listen to podcasts, connect with other Frommers.com members through our active-reader forums, share your travel photos, read blogs from guidebook editors and fellow travelers, and much more.

A Note on Prices

In the "Take a Break" and "Best Bets" sections of this book, we have used a system of dollar signs to show a range of costs for 1 night in a hotel (the price of a double-occupancy room) or the cost of an entree at a restaurant. Use the following table to decipher the dollar signs:

Cost	Hotels	Restaurants
$	under $130	under $15
$$	$130–$200	$15–$30
$$$	$200–$300	$30–$40
$$$$	$300–$395	$40–$50
$$$$$	over $395	over $50

How to Contact Us

In researching this book, we discovered many wonderful places—hotels, restaurants, shops, and more. We're sure you'll find others. Please tell us about them, so we can share the information with your fellow travelers in upcoming editions. If you were disappointed with a recommendation, we'd love to know that, too. Please write to: Support@FrommerMedia.com

17 Favorite
Moments

17 Favorite Moments

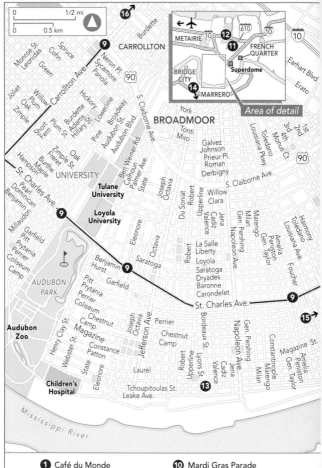

1 Café du Monde
2 Jackson Square
3 Frenchmen Street
4 Ferry to Algiers
5 Preservation Hall
6 Napoleon House
7 Louisiana Music Factory
8 National World War II Museum
9 St. Charles streetcar
10 Mardi Gras Parade
   (not mapped; see p. 28)
11 Liuzza's by the Track
12 City Park
13 Hansen's Sno-Bliz
14 Swamp Tour
15 Commander's Palace
16 Mid-City Rock 'n' Bowl
17 Faulkner House Books

Previous page: Jackson Square with the Cabildo, St. Louis Cathedral, and the Presbytère (from left to right) in the background.

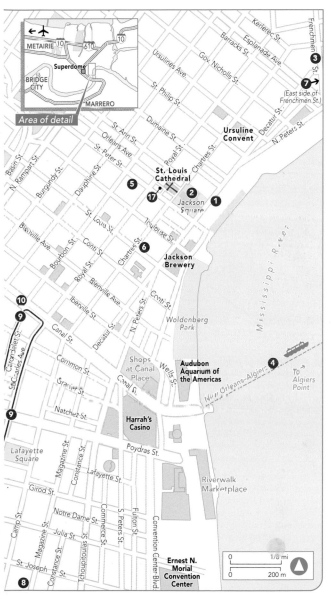

It's true that romance is in the air in New Orleans—the air *itself* is dewy, dreamy perfumed. Perhaps that's why, in your first few breaths here, the irresistible city entrances you to fall in love with it. It could be the undeniable, unchanged beauty of the French Quarter and the Garden District, where history is alive right beneath your feet. Maybe it's the deeply embedded groove of centuries of music flowing from doorways, street corners, and clubs. Perhaps it's because of the stunning old masters, modernists, and bohemian street artists filling the city's museums and galleries. Or simply because of the non-stop *partay* (the place has an *official cocktail*, after all). It's where gumbo—the savory Creole stew that is often (over) used in describing the multicultural tableau here—is actually an apt metaphor for a place that's deep and mysterious, rich with flavor and spiked with spice, and so much more than the sum of its many disparate parts. Unique, beloved New Orleans works its charms like a spell. See, hear, and taste for yourself, starting with these favorite moments, and let New Orleans cast its seductive spell on you.

First beignet bite at Café du Monde.

❶ **Your first beignet bite at world-famous Café du Monde.** The fryer-fresh trio of delight is positively doused in powdered sugar (as you too will soon be). Add a creamy café au lait and the heaps of atmosphere at this 150-year-old locale, and you've got so much more than a doughnut. *See p 46.*

❷ **People-watch in Jackson Square.** The French Quarter's beating heart pulses night and day with talented street musicians, eclectic artists, colorful fortune-tellers, and the tourists ogling them. Join them—it's a free show (well, drop a buck in the hat if you take in the entertainment). *See p 47.*

❸ **Club-hop along Frenchmen Street.** Stroll the dozen-plus nightclubs along this three-block stretch and check out the sounds and scenes—inside and out—until you find one, or three, that strike your fancy. Cover charges are usually affordable (or non-existent), and you can find something for every ear. *See p 11.*

❹ **Take a sunset ferry across the Mississippi River to Algiers Point.** It's a cheap and easy way to go rolling on the river, and offers a

Passengers aboard the ferry to Algiers Point enjoy views of the New Orleans skyline.

Napoleon House in the French Quarter.

dramatic view of the city skyline. *See p 165.*

5 Finally "get" the whole trad jazz thing at Preservation Hall. This is the real thing, people, played by superb musicians in a tiny, crumbling room with no amplification or clinking glasses. It's all about the bass (and drums and horns and piano), just like a century ago when this music first blew minds. *See p 119.*

6 Toast the summer year-round with a Pimm's Cup at Napoleon House. The 200-year-old mansion where France's exiled Little Corporal very nearly lived makes a perfect backdrop for the gin-and-cuke house specialty. Savor it with a hot muffaletta sandwich in the dark cafe or sweet courtyard, as you mingle amid local artisans and curious tourists. *See p 115.*

7 Flip through vinyl while tapping toes at Louisiana Music Factory. The beloved indie record store on Frenchmen Street has a stellar selection of local music—and musicians, who play showcase sets most Saturdays. The new and used selection emphasizes jazz, blues, R & B, Cajun, zydeco, and swamp pop. *See p 80.*

8 Climb into a Higgins landing craft at the National World War II Museum. The boat that made victory possible on D-Day was invented and built in New Orleans.

The museum that grew (and grew and grew) around it is an astounding must-do. *See p 37.*

9 Ride the ultra-scenic St. Charles streetcar. Clackety-clack up world-famous St. Charles Avenue and ogle the elegant historic mansions and renowned universities. You'll veritably feel history in the worn-smooth wooden seats and the breeze through the windows as the iconic green cars clamber beneath a sweeping canopy of live oaks. *See p 165.*

10 Yell, "Throw me something, mistah!" at a Mardi Gras parade— till your neck can't sustain another strand and your loot bag is full of doubloons and throws. Then you'll realize that it's really about the camaraderie, float decor, resolute flambeaux, ingenious costumes, marching bands' precision, general hilarity, and decades of storied tradition behind it all. *See p 29.*

A ride on the St. Charles streetcar is a fun and cheap way to get a passing view of the Garden District.

No one can resist a snoball from Hansen's Sno-Bliz.

⓫ Savor the sandwiches and repartee at Liuzza's by the Track. Good poor boy shops abound citywide. This one, in the charming Bayou St. John neighborhood, attracts locals as flavorful as the gumbo. We favor a cup of it plus half a garlic oyster poor boy, with an icy Abita Amber, natch. *See p 105.*

⓬ Spend a day in City Park. Three times the size of Central Park with something for everyone: pedal boating, a stunning sculpture garden, swans floating on serene ponds, a kid-sized train and amusement park, golf, romantic picnic spots, bike rentals, and abounding, beautifully landscaped open space and photo ops. Oh, and beignets. *See p 82.*

⓭ Cool off with a snoball at Hansen's Sno-Bliz. No slushies or slurpies here! The ice shaving machines invented here make for a uniquely divine fluffiness, and its house-made syrups elicit endless sweet or sour combinations. Now run by the third generation, it's a seasonal local ritual that's worth the wait. *See p 103.*

⓮ Take a spooky swamp tour and freak out at the wide-mouthed gators. The utterly distinctive, primordial environs are more beautiful than you might expect, and the gators get up close and personal so you can check out those serious chompers. *See p 89.*

⓯ Indulge in a swank, 3-hour meal at Commander's Palace. Okay, it's more than a moment. But the long, lingering, diet-to-the-wind, boozy blowout dinner at one of the city's classic old restaurants is a *de rigueur* New Orleans experience. You can't go wrong at Commander's. *See p 100.*

⓰ Bowl to live zydeco music at Mid-City Rock 'n' Bowl. Shouldn't there be a bowling alley where you can two-step to a raucous zydeco or swing band between frames in every town? No, there shouldn't. It should *only* be in New Orleans. The first and best of its kind still is. *See p 116.*

⓱ Browse the storied shelves at Faulkner House Books. This elegant, intimate bookstore alongside St. Louis Cathedral (in a townhouse where the Pulitzer Prize–winning author once lived and wrote) is a reader's dream, with rare first editions, best sellers, and a wonderful selection of works by local authors. *See p 76.* ●

Mid-City Rock 'n' Bowl.

1 The Best Full-Day Tours

The Best **in One Day**

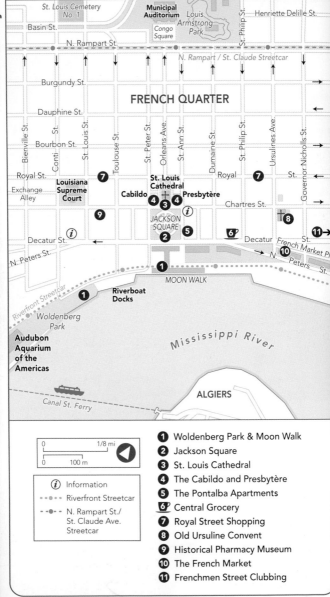

1. Woldenberg Park & Moon Walk
2. Jackson Square
3. St. Louis Cathedral
4. The Cabildo and Presbytère
5. The Pontalba Apartments
6. Central Grocery
7. Royal Street Shopping
8. Old Ursuline Convent
9. Historical Pharmacy Museum
10. The French Market
11. Frenchmen Street Clubbing

Previous page: A trumpet player blows his horn in front of St. Louis Cathedral.

The vibrant 300-year-old Vieux Carré ("Old Square"), with its endless eyefuls of florid architecture, copious cultural oddities, and stories that seem to emanate from the very streets, looks much like it did when it was founded in 1718. If you have only 1 day in New Orleans, spend it here, in the world-famous heart of the city. Walk under wrought-iron balconies, peer down brick-lined walkways to steal glances of impressive private courtyards, stop and toe-tap to a trio of crazy-good street musicians (and leave them a few bucks). Cool off in an ancient looking bar and, "go-cup" in hand, search the shops for the perfect souvenir trinket. START: Woldenberg Park, across from Jackson Square.

A sign in Jackson Square noting the former Spanish name of the square, Plaza de Armas.

① 🚶 **Woldenberg Park and Moon Walk.** Take in the rolling Mississippi River, public artworks, and maybe a busking sax player as you stroll the sleepy waterside park. The Moon Walk, a landing overlooking Jackson Square, is named for former mayor Maurice Edwin "Moon" Landrieu. 🕐 *20 min. Across from Jackson Square along Mississippi River.*

② ★★★ 🧒 **Jackson Square.** In the days when it was known as the Plaza de Armas, military parades and public executions were held here. On November 30, 1803, citizens gathered here to learn that Louisiana was once again a French possession. Weeks later, the Louisiana Purchase returned it to America, in the cheapest and largest land grab of all time. These days it's the town square, where artists display paintings, fortune tellers read palms, and the view is as unforgettable as it was way back then. 🕐 *30 min.–1 hr. Fronts the 700 block of Decatur St. and is bounded by Chartres, St. Ann, and St. Peter sts. Dawn–dusk.*

③ ★★ **St. Louis Cathedral.** The oldest continuously operating cathedral in the U.S., and the center of the city's large Catholic population, this is the third building on this spot. A 1722 hurricane demolished the first, and the Good Friday fire of 1788 burned the second. 🕐 *20 min. 615 Pere Antoine Alley. 504/525-9585. www.stlouis cathedral.org. Mon–Sat 8:30am–4pm, Sun 9am–2pm. Mass schedule online.*

St. Louis Cathedral.

Historical Pharmacy Museum.

④ ★★ The Cabildo and Presbytère. Flanking the cathedral, this excellent history museum (housing Napoleon's death mask) was built in 1795 as the Spanish seat of government; in 1803 the French turned over Louisiana to the U.S. here. To the cathedral's right, the matching **Presbetère** was erected as the never-used home for church clergy, now with its hurricane and Mardi Gras exhibits. ⏲ 1 hr. 701 Chartres St. ☎ 800/568-6968 or 504/568-6968. www.louisiana statemuseum.org/museums. Admission $6 adults; $5 students, seniors, and active military; children 12 and under free. Tues–Sun 10am–4:30pm.

⑤ ★★ Pharmacy Museum. They've got leeches, snake oil potions, opium bottles, and torturous-looking antique surgical instruments. The slightly gruesome guided tour of this apothecary shop, site of the first licensed pharmacist in the U.S. (dating to 1823), is fascinating. ⏲ 1 hr. 514 Chartres St.

☎ 504/565-8027. www.pharmacy museum.org. $5 adults, $4 students and seniors; children 5 and under free. Tues–Sat 10am–4pm. Guided tours Tues–Fri 1pm. Closes early for private events some Saturdays—call ahead.

⑥ ★ The Pontalba Apartments. The elegant, Creole European–style buildings alongside Jackson Square (and the square itself) were built by Baroness Pontalba as an early show of (girl) power when the American Sector, across Canal Street, was expanding. Pontalba, whose rich and powerful daddy Don Almonester rebuilt St. Louis Cathedral, left her mark in the cast-iron railing: look for the entwined "A.P." initials. The second-story apartments remain coveted real estate today. ⏲ 30 min. 523 St. Ann St. ☎ 504/524-9118. www.louisianastate museum.org/museums/1850-house. Tues–Sun 10am–4:30pm. Admission $3 adults; $2 students, seniors, and active military; children 12 and under free.

7 Central Grocery. It's a complete Italian deli but what you want is a muffuletta, the famously filling round sandwich packed with cold cuts, cheese, and olive salad. One feeds many (and yes, they ship). *923 Decatur St.* ☎ *504/523-1620. $.*

8 200–1000 blocks of Royal Street. Antiques and boutiques, galleries and live art abound—one of the best streets anywhere for window shoppers or serious collectors buying—while a band of 20-somethings plays 1920s jazz on the sidewalk. For a detailed map of shops along Royal Street, turn to p 73. ⏱ *90 min.*

9 ★★ Old Ursuline Convent. Built in 1752 as a convent and school for girls by French nuns of the Sisters of Ursula order, it houses local Catholic archives dating to 1718. It may be best known for populating New Orleans with a long line of good girls (a rare commodity in the lawless, burgeoning city back then). ⏱ *1–1½ hr. 1100 Chartres St.* ☎ *504/529-3040. www.stlouiscathedral.org/convent-museum. Admission $5 adults, $4 seniors, $3 students; children 6 and under free. Mon–Fri 10am–4pm; Sat 9am–3pm.*

10 ★★ The French Market. This open-air, European-style market has been here for well over 200 years. Today it has a farmers' market, food booths, arty-crafty goods, and flea market stalls with souvenirs. Stop for a nosh, a trinket, or a

Preparing the famous muffuletta sandwiches at Central Grocery.

cooking demo, recalling that once upon a time, pirates hawked their booty right here. ⏱ *45 min. Decatur St. between Ursulines and Barracks sts.* ☎ *504/522-2621. www.frenchmarket.org. Free admission. Daily 9am–6pm.*

11 ★★★ Frenchmen Street Clubbing. About a dozen clubs reside within 3 blocks, each with its own vibe and live music line-up from a grubby bar with lowdown blues to an upscale, sit-down room with leading jazzmen. A street full of music lovers, scenesters, and characters soak it all up. This is where you want to be at night. *Frenchmen St. between Decatur and Royal sts. Covers vary from free to $20 (more for special events).*

The Best **in Two Days**

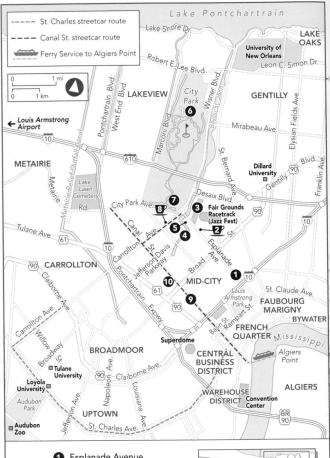

- - - - - St. Charles streetcar route
- - - - - Canal St. streetcar route
🚢 Ferry Service to Algiers Point

0 — 1 mi
0 — 1 km

Lake Pontchartrain

LAKE OAKS

University of New Orleans

Lake Shore Dr.

Robert E. Lee Blvd.

Leon C. Simon Dr.

GENTILLY

← Louis Armstrong Airport

LAKEVIEW

City Park ❻

Mirabeau Ave.

Elysian Fields Ave.

METAIRIE

Lake Lawn Cemetery Rd.

Dillard University

Gentilly Blvd.

Franklin Ave.

Desaix Blvd.

❼

City Park Ave. ❽

❸ Fair Grounds Racetrack (Jazz Fest)

❺
❹
❷

Tulane Ave.

CARROLLTON

Canal Ave.

Esplanade Ave.

Broad St.

❶

St. Claude Ave.

FAUBOURG MARIGNY

❿ MID-CITY

BYWATER

Jefferson Davis Parkway

Louis Armstrong Park

FRENCH QUARTER

❾

Basin St.

Rampart St.

Mississippi

Algiers Point

BROADMOOR

Superdome

CENTRAL BUSINESS DISTRICT

ALGIERS

Tulane University

Loyola University

Audubon Park

UPTOWN

WAREHOUSE DISTRICT

Convention Center

BR 90

Audubon Zoo

St. Charles Ave.

❶ Esplanade Avenue
❷ Café Degas
❸ St. Louis Cemetery No. 3
❹ Bayou St. John
❺ Pitot House
❻ City Park
❼ New Orleans Museum of Art
❽ Toup's Meatery
❾ Canal Streetcar
❿ Chickie Wah Wah

✈ KENNER   METAIRIE   610

Superdome

BRIDGE CITY

WESTWEGO

Area of detail

History, scenery, action, and architecture—you'll fit it all in during a day perusing Esplanade Ridge, Bayou St. John, City Park, and environs. These aren't the best-known sections of the city, but you'll explore some significant landmarks and attractions, and get a good feel for what a typical neighborhood is like. Try to detour down some side streets, too. START: **The 800 block of Esplanade Avenue (at Bourbon Street).**

❶ ★★ **Esplanade Avenue.** A ride, long walk, or slow drive up Esplanade, a lush boulevard of stately homes and seemingly ancient trees stretching overhead, allows for a gander at some gorgeous and notable properties (and some, not so much). This area was Creole society's less grand, more approachable answer to Uptown's St. Charles Avenue. ⏱ 30–60 min. 800–3300 Esplanade Ave.

St. Louis Cemetery No. 3.

❷ **Café Degas.** This charming, romantic, French bistro serves a perfect salad Niçoise and has a tree growing in the middle of its indoor/outdoor dining room. All that atmosphere plus excellent omelets and traditional favorites—a great brunch, lunch, or dinner spot. Reserve ahead. 3127 Esplanade Ave. www.cafedegas.com. ☎ 504/945-5635. $$.

❸ ★★ **St Louis Cemetery No. 3.** A fine example of New Orleans's famous "Cities of the Dead," where elaborate marble family tombs encircled by cast-iron fencing are watched over by weeping stone angels. This cemetery was built over a former burial ground for

A beautifully restored house on Esplanade Avenue.

Enjoying the afternoon on Bayou St. John.

lepers. ⏱ *60 min. 3421 Esplanade Ave.* ☎ *504/482-5065. www.nola catholiccemeteries.org. Free admission. Mon–Sat 9am–3pm, Sun 9am–4pm (holiday closings vary).*

Head back to Esplanade, and when you reach Moss Street, turn left and walk along the west side of Bayou St. John.

④ ★ Bayou St. John. This once-bustling, historic waterway connecting Lake Pontchartrain to the Mississippi River, served as an important trading channel for Native Americans and, later, a stealthy bypass that influenced European explorers to found the city at this site. Now it's a peaceful, meandering waterway and a scenic spot popular with picnickers and paddlers. (We love Kayakitiyat tours; see p 85.) ⏱ *30 min.*

⑤ ★ Pitot House. The romantic grounds, period furnishings, and excellent docents at this Creole colonial house turned museum will help you imagine life as an early New Orleans settler, when many such "country houses" and plantation owners' homes fronted the Bayou. Dating from 1799, the city's first American mayor, James Pitot, resided here from 1810 to 1819. ⏱ *1 hr. 1440 Moss St.* ☎ *504/482-0312. www.pitothouse.org. Admission $10 adults, $7 students, seniors, and children 6–17; children under 6 free. Wed–Sat 10am–3pm.*

Double-back on Moss Street, and cross the Bayou via Magnolia Bridge, the 1936 WPA-built steel structure. Turn right along the east side of the Bayou.

⑥ ★★★ kids City Park. City Park is without doubt one of the nation's finest urban parks—1,300 acres of beautifully landscaped just about everything, including the largest collection of moss-draped live oaks in the world. The park offers boating, biking, golf, tennis, mini-golf, a kid-sized amusement park, carousel equestrian trails, a scale-model ride-aboard train, a model train garden, stunning sculpture gardens, botanical gardens, and acres of space for running, walking, or just soaking it all in. And did we mention swans? Or beignets? ⏱ *1 hr. 1 Palm Dr.; bounded by City Park Ave. and Canal, Lee, and Wisner boulevards.* ☎ *504/482-4888. www.neworleanscitypark.com. Free admission. Open daily.*

⑦ ★★★ New Orleans Museum of Art. City Park's main oak-lined entrance also leads directly to NOMA, by turns classical and modern in architecture and collection—and both are stunning. The superbly curated exhibits—from priceless old master oils to avant garde photographs—are always worth a visit. ⏱ *2–3 hr. 1 Collins Diboll Circle.* ☎ *504/658-4100. www.noma.org. Admission $10.50 adults, $8.50 seniors and students with I.D., $6.50 children 7–12, free for children 6 and under. Tues–Thurs 10am–6pm; Fri 10am–9pm; Sat 10am–5pm; Sun 11am–5pm.*

⑧ ★★ Toups' Meatery. Hearty country meets sophisticated city in the beefy, porky goodness here, earning Chef Toups two James Beard Award nominations. Start with the house-cured charcuterie.

New Orleans Museum of Art.

Non-red-meat eaters should get the chicken thigh confit; everyone gets the doberge cake, 845 N. Carrollton Ave. www.toupsmeatery.com. ☎ 504/252-4999. $$. Closed Sun–Mon.

⑨ ★★ kids Canal Streetcar.
Unlike the streetcars of the historic St. Charles line, the newer Canal cars are bright red, air conditioned, and wheelchair accessible. They might lack the, um, character of antiquation, but that cool air feels good on a humid afternoon. The track running from City Park east along Carrollton Avenue hangs a Louie at Canal Street, heading back

toward the French Quarter and Central Business District. ① *30 min. Carrollton Ave. at Orleans Ave.* ☎ *504/827-7970. www.norta.com. $1.25 one-way fare. See p 165.*

Hop off at White Street and cross Canal Street to end the day at one of the city's coolest clubs.

⑩ ★★★ Chickie Wah Wah.
At this Mid-City nightclub, consistently solid local roots, rock, blues, and singer-songwriter bookings draw reverent crowds. The clean, midsize, shotgun-style room is decorated with cool old tin signs. ① *1–3 hours. 2828 Canal St. (at N. White St.). www.chickiewahwah.com.* ☎ *504/304-4714. Cover $8–$20.*

Chickie Wah Wah.

The Best **in Three Days**

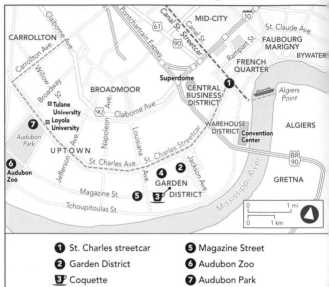

1 St. Charles streetcar
2 Garden District
3 Coquette
4 Lafayette Cemetery No. 1
5 Magazine Street
6 Audubon Zoo
7 Audubon Park

Strolling the architecturally astounding Garden District, you may think you've entered an entirely separate city—or time period—from the French Quarter. Although once a separate city (Lafayette) and established later than the French Quarter, their development by two different groups is what most profoundly distinguishes them. The French Quarter was settled by Creoles during the French and Spanish colonial periods; the Garden District was created by Americans after the 1803 Louisiana Purchase. This itinerary also side-steps to eclectic restaurants and boutiques along Magazine Street: hello, foodies and shoppers. START: **Canal and Carondelet streets or any stop along the route following St. Charles and Carrollton avenues.**

---

1 ★★★ kids St. Charles Streetcar. From 1835 to 1893, the St. Charles line was mule-driven. The present streetcars are listed on the National Register of Historic Places, and a ride along this capital-A Avenue truly feels like a step back in time. If you have more than three people in your party and the streetcar isn't full, you can pull the back of one wooden bench so that two benches face one another for a cozy tête-à-tête. ⏲ 30 min.–2 hr. ☎ 504/827-8300. www.norta.com. $1.25 one-way fare.

❷ ★★★ Garden District. It's practically required that you tour this impressive area, one of the glories of the city. You'll be awed by the lush gardens and massive estates. Originally created by the nouveau riche who weren't welcome in Creole society, let's not forget that much of it was built on the literal backs of slave labor, from which that wealth was derived. ⏱ 90 min. Bounded by Magazine St. and St. Charles, Jackson, and Louisiana aves. See p 52.

A ride on the St. Charles streetcar should be on every visitor's to-do list.

❸ ★★★ Coquette. The cuisine at this smart, polished bistro remains consistently adventurous without being haughty or hoity. The atmosphere is chic but comfortable. A personal favorite for lunch, dinner, or in between. 2800 Magazine St. www.coquettenola. com. ☎ 504/265-0421. $$.

❹ ★ Lafayette Cemetery No. 1. Established in 1833, this well-restored "city of the dead" is one of New Orleans's oldest cemeteries. Tombs typically house numerous corpses from an extended family—one lists 37 entrants—others are designated for members of fire

departments or fraternal organizations. Civil War soldier friends are buried in one corner, and author Anne Rice's characters make frequent appearances here. ⏱ 30 min. 1400 block of Washington Ave. ☎ 504/525-3377, www.saveourcemeteries. org. Tour (with online reservation) $15 adults, children under 12 free. Add $5 for walk-ups, if space is available. Daily tour 10:30am. Closed some holidays. See p 53.

❺ ★★ Magazine Street. Shopaholics could spend all day perusing the 6 miles (9.6km) of antiques shops, clothing and home-decor boutiques, art galleries, and restaurants. There's a welcome mix of the junky, the funky, and the very

The shops along Magazine Street.

Streetcar Dollars & Sense

The streetcar fare is $1.25 each way. Exact change is required if paying onboard. Or you can pre-purchase a **Jazzy Pass** for unlimited rides on streetcars or buses at $3 for 1 day, $9 for 3 days, or $15 for 5 days. (There's a slightly higher Jazzy Pass option that includes rides on the Algiers Ferry; see p 165.) Passes are available at local Walgreens (except the 5-day pass) and at the transit shelters at Canal and N. Peters streets or Canal and Bourbon streets. Better yet, purchase and display the Jazzy Pass on your smartphone with the handy **RTA GoMobile** app. For more info, contact the **New Orleans Regional Transit Authority** (☎ 504/248-3900; www.norta.com).

au courant. Prime sections include blocks 1900–2100, 3700–4300, and 5400–5700. ⏱ *2–3 hr. Bookended by Canal St. and Audubon Park.*

6 kids **Audubon Zoo.** As zoos go, this one is larger than you'd expect, yet still plenty charming. Among the 1,800 animals are many subtropical species that flourish in the city's heat and humidity. A mini water park is a great diversion for kids visiting in the warmer months. ⏱ *3 hr. 6500 Magazine St. See p 91.*

7 ★★★ kids **Audubon Park.** This sprawling park is great for bird-watching along a lagoon or boat-watching on "The Fly" green space overlooking the Mississippi. Great for runners or families looking for playground time. For sporting types, there's golf and tennis. ⏱ *45 min. 6500 St. Charles Ave. (across from Tulane and Loyola universities, btw. St. Charles Ave. & Magazine St.).* ☎ *504/581-4629. Daily 5am–10pm. See p 90.* ●

The grand oak trees in Audubon Park.

2 The Best Special-Interest Tours

Cemeteries: Cities of the Dead

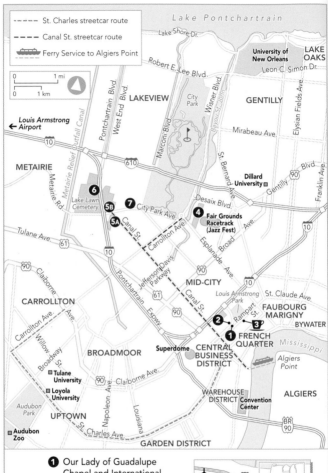

- - - - St. Charles streetcar route
- - - - Canal St. streetcar route

🛳 Ferry Service to Algiers Point

① Our Lady of Guadalupe Chapel and International Shrine of St. Jude

② St. Louis Cemetery No. 1

③ Mister Gregory's

④ St. Louis Cemetery No. 3

⑤A Cypress Grove Cemetery

⑤B Greenwood Cemetery

⑥ Lake Lawn Metairie Cemetery

⑦ Holt Cemetery

Area of detail

Previous page: Mardi Gras parades through the streets of New Orleans.

New Orleans's famous "Cities of the Dead" are both impressive and practical. Many believe that traditional underground graves were eschewed due to the city's high water table. Their similarity to the famed Père-Lachaise cemetery in Paris, though, lends credence to some historians' insistence that the above-ground tombs were merely built in the French and Spanish tradition. Learning the details of the mourning traditions and burial practices (what exactly happens inside those tombs, anyway?) is quite fascinating, so taking a professional cemetery tour is well worth it (and that's the only way to get into St. Louis No. 1, so be sure to book one in advance). All of these cemeteries are still in use, so keep in mind that these are sacred places, worthy of respect. Marking or otherwise vandalizing tombs, or taking souvenirs, is both insolent and illegal. Also see Lafayette Cemetery No. 1, p 53. This tour crosses town to view both famous and lesser-known cemeteries. A Jazzy Pass (p 165) and a good pair of walking shoes will get you to all of them in a day. START: **Our Lady of Guadalupe Chapel, 411 N. Rampart St., at the edge of the French Quarter.**

❶ ★ Our Lady of Guadalupe Chapel and International Shrine of St. Jude.

The small chapel was built in 1826 (preceding the more famous and grand St. Louis Cathedral by a quarter century) as a funeral church for the many victims of consecutive yellow fever epidemics. Today, many visitors travel a great distance to pray to Jude, patron saint of hopeless and impossible cases, as a last resort to heal terminal illness. The spooky-cool, candlelit chapel is laden with their prayer placards. ⓘ 20 min. 411 N. Rampart St. ☎ 504/525-1551. www.judeshrine. com. Donations welcome. Gift shop Mon–Sat 9am–5pm. Masses daily starting at 7am.

Our Lady of Guadalupe Chapel.

❷ ★★ St. Louis Cemetery No. 1.

Opened in 1789 (most of the French Quarter burned the year before), the site is the resting place of such celebrated locals as the city's first mayor, Etienne de Boré; civil rights pioneer Homer Plessy; New Orleans's first African-American mayor, Ernest "Dutch" Morial; and world-champion chess player Paul Morphy. The most popular landmark is the Glapion family crypt, where revered (and feared) voodoo priestess Marie Laveau (p 59) was supposedly laid to rest. Some uneducated followers mark her tomb with three small Xs, supposedly so that she will grant them a wish—a false tradition. Needless to say, desecrating any tomb is absolutely forbidden. Visitors allowed in only with a licensed tour guide. ⓘ 90 min. Conti & Basin sts. ☎ 504/525-3377. www.saveourcemeteries.org.

Tour $20 adults, kids 12 and under free. Tours Mon–Sat 10am, 11:30am, 1pm; Sun 10am. Meet at Our Lady of Guadalupe Church (above). Closed holidays.

Walk 1 block south to Rampart Street; go left for 5 blocks.

3 **Mister Gregory's.** Take a break from the dead and revive with some French press coffee and a decadent pain perdu muffin, gooey with crème Anglaise. Hearty onion soup, salads, croque sandwiches, and all-day breakfasts round out a menu of simple, French-accented goodness. *806 N. Rampart St. www.mistergregorys.com.* ☎ *504/407-3780. $. Thurs–Mon 9am–10pm; Tues–Wed 9am–4pm.*

Just left of Mister Gregory's is St. Ann Street. From there, take the #91 bus to St. Louis No. 3.

4 **★★ St. Louis Cemetery No. 3.** Imposing cast-iron gates usher you inside, where you'll find dramatic angel sculptures and elaborate above-ground tombs for some of the city's most distinguished Creole families. Established in 1854, the cemetery first opened 1 year after the city's worst yellow fever epidemic, and filled quickly. Look for tombs of prominent local figures such as legendary Storyville photographer Ernest Bellocq; free person of color and philanthropist Thomy Lafon, who left $600,000 to charity; and architect James Gallier, Jr. He designed the centograph for his tomb, which memorializes his Irish-born architect father, James Gallier, Sr., and his stepmother who perished when their steamship sank on its journey to New Orleans. The active, clean, well-maintained cemetery has a waiting list for burial space. ① *90 min. See p 65.*

Walk up Esplanade to Carrollton Avenue and take the Canal Streetcar to Canal Street. Transfer to the Cemeteries line, and take it to City Park Avenue. Turn right on City Park Avenue and walk half a block to the entrance to Cypress Grove Cemetery. The entrance to Greenwood, which is visible across the street, is a long block north on Canal Street.

5 **★★ Cypress Grove & Greenwood cemeteries.** These neighboring cemeteries were both founded in the mid-1800s by the Firemen's Charitable and Benevolent Association. Each has some highly original tombs; look for the ones made entirely of iron. Greenwood houses New Orleans's first Civil War memorial and the tomb of locally beloved, Pulitzer Prize–winning novelist John Kennedy Toole, of A Confederacy of Dunces fame. ① *1 hr. 120 City Park Ave. and 5200 Canal St.*

Hoof or taxi it west on City Park Avenue. Go under the expressway, and turn right on Pontchartrain Boulevard toward the next cemetery's entrance (about ¾ mile).

The supposed tomb of Marie Laveau at St. Louis Cemetery No. 1.

St. Louis Cemetery No. 3.

❻ ★ Lake Lawn Metairie Cemetery

The story goes that Charles T. Howard, a "new money" Yankee, was denied membership at an exclusive racetrack. He exacted revenge by purchasing the property, demolishing the track, and building this opulent, "youthful" graveyard (born in just 1872). Howard's tomb is here, along with such notables as bandleader Louis Prima; Popeye's Chicken fast-food chain founder Al Copeland; and Ruth Fertel of Ruth's Chris Steak House (whose marble edifice oddly resembles a piece of beef). Don't miss the pyramid-and-sphinx Brunswig mausoleum, the "ruined castle" Egan family tomb, and the Morales tomb. The former resting place of Storyville madam Josie Arlington has a statue of a girl knocking on a door—a virgin being turned away from Josie's brothel, some said, as Madam Josie would despoil none. The custom crypt was sold and her body moved when either it became a tourist attraction, or blue-blood families complained at having to "mix" with someone of Josie's ilk. Pick your explanation. ⏱ 90 min. 5100 Pontchartrain Blvd. ☎ 504/486-6331. www.lakelawnmetairie.com. Free admission. Daily 9am–4pm. Closed holidays.

Double-back toward Greenwood. At Canal Street and City Park Avenue, continue a half-mile, or take the #27 or #60 bus east on City Park for two stops to Conti Street. Cross City Park Avenue and turn on tiny Rosedale Drive (across from Burger King, next to Delgado Community College).

❼ ★★ Holt Cemetery

For the more intrepid (and truly cemetery-obsessed), this lesser-known graveyard is worth seeking out. Dating to the mid 1800s, this former burial ground for indigents has nearly all in-ground graves—unusual for New Orleans. They are maintained to varying degrees by the families, which results in its particular, folk art appeal, with hand drawn markers and family memorabilia scattered about. It's incredibly picturesque and poignant in its own way. ⏱ 30 min. 635 City Park Ave. Mon–Fri 8am–2:30pm, Sat 8am–noon.

Monument in Greenwood Cemetery.

New Orleans Literati

1 Ignatius J. Reilly statue
2 Hotel Monteleone
3 Antoine's
4 LeMonnier Mansion
5 Bourbon Orleans Hotel
6 Faulkner House
7 Tennessee Williams House
8 Victor David House
9 Pontalba Apartments

ⓘ Information
•••• Riverfront Streetcar
- - •- - N. Rampart St./
St. Claude Ave.
Streetcar

0 ——— 1/8 mi
0 ——— 100 m

New Orleans is renowned for its lack of moderation. Its literary history—laden with both luminaries and lesser-knowns—follows the pattern. For centuries, notable writers have been drawn to the city, where freedom of thought (and action) have always been revered; where the colorful history, eccentric characters, and sensual charms inspire ideation; and where the city's contrasts—beauty and decay, rich and poor—kick-start the imagination. This leisurely walking tour of the French Quarter highlights a few literary hot spots. START: **800 Iberville St.**

❶ Ignatius J. Reilly statue.

John Kennedy Toole's New Orleans–set novel *A Confederacy of Dunces* went unseen until 11 years after his 1969 suicide. His mother tirelessly shopped the manuscript. It was finally published—and won a Pulitzer Prize. Some believe that the idiosyncratic Ignatius, the indolent, urbane protagonist immortalized here, epitomizes many a French Quarter character. *800 Iberville St.*

Walk down Iberville Street to Royal Street and turn left.

❷ ★★ Hotel Monteleone. The
venerable hotel is ground zero of New Orleans' literati. The lengthy list of legends who stayed, wrote, and/or drank here includes Ernest

Ignatius J. Reilly statue.

Hemingway, William Faulkner, Tennessee Williams, Anne Rice, Eudora Welty, Richard Ford, Winston Groom, and John Grisham. Truman Capote was nearly born in a suite here (a late change of plans resulted in a nearby hospital birth, to Tru's eternal disappointment). Check out the display of famous books penned herein (just inside the front doors as you enter the glorious lobby), and try a classic cocktail on the slow-turning Carousel bar (p 141). *214 Royal St.*

Continue up Royal Street to St. Louis Street and turn left.

❸ ★★ Antoine's. One of the
first fine-dining restaurants in the New World, it's been owned and operated by the same family for an astonishing 175 years, during which the hoi polloi of New Orleans society, plus countless celebrities, have slurped down oysters Rockefeller (invented here) and partied down in the many private rooms. With its crisp, white-jacketed waitstaff and French-based cuisine, it's as classic as New Orleans gets. It's also a central character in Dinner at Antoine's, Frances Parkinson Keyes's best-selling murder mystery of 1948. *713 St. Louis St. www. antoines.com.* ☎ 504/581-4422. $$.

Go back to Royal Street and turn left. Walk 2 blocks to St. Peter Street.

4 Le Monnier Mansion. In addition to its architectural significance as the first four-story building, this "skyscraper" looms large in the city's literary history. George Washington Cable lived and set his 1873 story, "Sieur George" here; John and Lou Webb published works by William Burroughs, Jack Kerouac, Henry Miller, Allen Ginsberg, and Lawrence Ferlinghetti in their pioneering *Outsider* journal, as well as the first book of a young poet named Charles Bukowski. *640 Royal St., at the corner of St. Peter St.*

Continue up Royal Street 1 block to Orleans Street and turn left.

5 Bourbon Orleans Hotel. Site of the famous quadroon balls, where wealthy white men were introduced to potential mistresses: free women (and girls) of color who were one-fourth black (quadroon). The men negotiated placage arrangements with the young women's mothers, covering financial, educational, housing, and child support for the mistresses. Accounts of this unusual but accepted custom appear in many books, notably Anne Rice's *The Feast of All Saints,* Isabel Allende's *Island Beneath the Sea,* and *Old Creole Days* by George Washington Cable. *717 Orleans Ave.*

Turn back down Orleans Street and cross Royal Street to Pirate's Alley.

6 ★★★ The Faulkner House. William Faulkner, Nobel and Pulitzer Prize–winning author and true literary icon, wrote his debut novel, *Soldiers' Pay,* here. Faulkner lived, wrote, and entertained here during the height of French Quarter bohemia in the 1920s, when New Orleans's decadent ways attracted a steady influx of artists and writers. The pioneering current owners—themselves central figures on the area's literary scene—have lovingly

Books by William Faulkner on sale at Faulkner House Books.

restored this stunning 1840 town house, turning the first floor into one of the premier independent bookstores in the country: the tiny, perfect, Faulkner House Books. An elegantly curated collection of first editions, rarities, and contemporary literature adorns the floor-to-ceiling shelves of this petite gem. ○ *30 min. 624 Pirate's Alley. Bookstore:* ☎ *504/524-2940. www.faulkner housebooks.com or www.wordsand music.org. Free admission. Bookstore daily 10am–5:30pm. Closed Mardi Gras day.*

Back on Royal Street, return to St. Peter Street and turn left.

7 ★ Tennessee Williams House. Despite the (pen) name, Tennessee Williams may be the literary figure most closely associated with New Orleans, which the native Missourian considered his spiritual home. About *A Streetcar Named Desire,* which he wrote from an attic room here in 1946, Williams said that he could hear "that rattle trap streetcar named Desire running along Royal and the one named Cemeteries running along Canal, and it seemed the perfect metaphor

Beyond Vampires

New Orleans has inspired many to pick up the pen, and perhaps it will inspire you to pick up a book or three. Once you've conquered Anne Rice's fangtastic modern horror classic *Interview with the Vampire*, try John Kennedy Toole's offbeat, Pulitzer Prize–winning *A Confederacy of Dunces,* or one of James Lee Burke's page-turners featuring Cajun crime-buster Dave Robicheaux. The Tennessee Williams drama *A Streetcar Named Desire* captures the city's boozy, sweaty malaise like none other, while George Washington Cable's *Old Creole Days* poked fun at NOLA life circa 1879. For non-fiction, start with Ned Sublette's fascinating *The World That Made New Orleans* and work your way up to Gary Krist's *Empire of Sin: A Story of Sex, Jazz, Murder, and the Battle for Modern New Orleans.* Katrina spawned brilliant, moving analyses and memoirs, including *Why New Orleans Matters* by Tom Piazza and Dan Baum's *Nine Lives.* For dessert, feast on Sara Roahen's delightful *Gumbo Tales: Finding My Place at the New Orleans Table.*

for the human condition." *632 St. Peter St. No public admission.*

8 Victor David House. In 1838, wealthy merchant Victor David built this exquisite example of sophisticated Greek Revival styling. Nearly a century later, historian novelist Grace King purchased the property to serve as headquarters for Le Petit Salon, an influential ladies' club

Pontalba Apartments.

whose purpose was to preserve New Orleans and French Quarter culture. Combined with next door's **Le Petit Théâtre du Vieux Carré** (founded in 1916), this was a powerfully influential literary block. *620 St. Peter St. No public admission.*

9 ★★ Pontalba Apartments. Among the mid-1920s New Orleans salons, perhaps none was so soignée (if short-lived) than that of Sherwood Anderson. Somerset Maugham, Edna St. Vincent Millay, Carl Sandburg, William Faulkner (whom Anderson mentored), and others congregated in the Pontalba parlor overlooking beautiful Jackson Square. Some of the works that appeared in the influential *Double Dealer* literary journal likely originated here. The *Dealer,* founded to promote the oft-maligned Southern culture, brought acclaim to the emergent American modernist literary movement and gave rise to the *Southern Review. 540-B St. Peter St.*

Mardi Gras

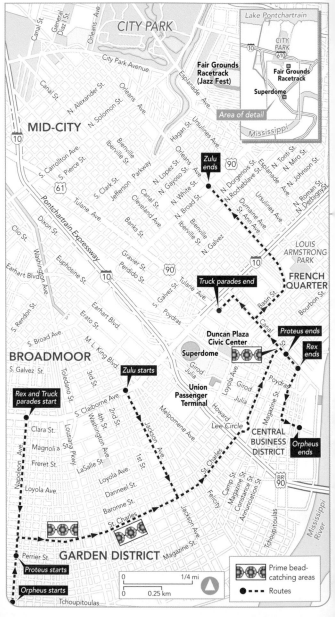

Lake Pontchartrain

CITY PARK

Fair Grounds Racetrack (Jazz Fest)

Fair Grounds Racetrack

Superdome

Area of detail

Mississippi

General Diaz St.

Canal St.

Orleans Ave.

City Park Ave.

Canal St.

MID-CITY

N. Alexander St.

N. Solomon St.

Orleans Ave.

Orleans Ave.

Ursulines Ave.

Hagan St.

Zulu ends

N. Dorgenois St.

Esplanade Ave.

N. Tonti St.

N. Miro St.

N. Johnson St.

S. Carrollton Ave.

S. Pierce St.

Bienville

Iberville St.

N. Lopez St.

N. Gayoso St.

N. White St.

N. Broad St.

N. Rocheblave St.

Ursulines Ave.

N. Roman St.

N. Derbigny St.

Tulane Ave.

Jefferson Parkway

S. Clark St.

Canal St.

Cleveland Ave.

Bienville

N. Iberville St.

N. Galvez

Dumaine Ave.

St. Ann Ave.

LOUIS ARMSTRONG PARK

Pontchartrain Expressway

Clio St.

Washington Ave.

Earhart Blvd.

Euphosine St.

Dixon St.

Banks St.

Gravier St.

Perdido St.

Tulane Ave.

S. Galvez St.

S. Poydras

Basin St.

Bourbon St.

FRENCH QUARTER

Truck parades end

S. Rendon St.

S. Broad Ave.

Erato St.

M. L. King Blvd.

Earhart Blvd.

Proteus ends

Canal St.

Rex ends

BROADMOOR

S. Galvez St.

Toledano Ave.

3rd St.

Zulu starts

Duncan Plaza Civic Center

Superdome

Girod
Julia

Union Passenger Terminal

Loyola Ave.

Girod

Julia

Poydras

Magazine St.

Rex and Truck parades start

Clara St.

Magnolia St.

Freret St.

S. Claiborne Ave.

4th St.

2nd St.

Louisiana Pkwy.

Washington Ave.

LaSalle St.

Loyola Ave.

Jackson Ave.

Melpomene Ave.

1st St.

Howard

Lee Circle

St. Charles

Camp St.

Magazine St.

Constance St.

Annunciation St.

CENTRAL BUSINESS DISTRICT

Orpheus ends

BR 90

Napoleon Ave.

Loyola Ave.

Danneel St.

Baronne St.

St. Charles

Jackson Ave.

Felicity

Tchoupitoulas

Mississippi River

Perrier St.

Proteus starts

GARDEN DISTRICT

Magazine St.

St. Charles

Orpheus starts

Tchoupitoulas

0   1/4 mi
0   0.25 km

Prime bead-catching areas

Routes

Mardi Gras—the biggest free party in North America—is New Orleans's most popular event, for good reason: the creativity, crowds, and camaraderie—not to mention the music, marching, and general merriment—and the memories you'll make. Despite the reputation, it's much more than a spring break–style drunkfest. It's a family event for locals and a celebration of traditions new and old, with religious origins: the old idea of good Christians massively indulging prior to their impending self-denial during Lent, the day after Mardi Gras. New Orleans's event dates to 1/43. By the mid-1800s, the elite **"krewes"** (groups of prominent society and business types) embraced it as the height of their social season. Today, those old-line (desegregated, finally) krewes and dozens of new ones keep the traditions, spectacle, hilarity, and subversion going. The largest parades have dozens of floats, celebrity guests, bands, dance troupes, scooter squads, and thousands of participants. You bring the rollicking, party-ready attitude; New Orleans does the rest.

Below are recommended events for Lundi Gras (Mon) and Mardi Gras (Tues); citywide parades roll nearly every day in the 2 weeks prior to Mardi Gras day.

A float from the Zulu Aid and Pleasure Club.

Lundi Gras (Monday)

❶ ★★ **Zulu Lundi Gras Festival.** Here's your opportunity to get a little pre-parade festing in—with three stages of music plus food and drinks along the riverfront, sponsored by Zulu. The big event comes around 5pm when the Zulu and Rex krewe kings arrive, welcomed by the mayor, who proclaims the official start of Mardi Gras. Afterward you can hightail it to the nearby part of the parade route on Canal Street to catch the Proteus parade (starts at 5:15pm), followed by Orpheus (see below). *www.lundi grasfestival.com. Woldenberg Park. Lundi Gras (Mon). 10am–6:30pm.*

❷ ★★★ **Orpheus.** Native New Orleanian Harry Connick, Jr.'s newish (1993) superkrewe boasts more than 1,200 men and women on 30 megafloats, throwing beads, pearls, silver doubloons, plush ducks, go-cups, and more. Celebrity guests serving as "royalty" have included Whoopi Goldberg, Sandra Bullock, Stevie Wonder, Quentin Tarantino, Dan Aykroyd, and James Brown, the "Godfather of Soul." *www. kreweoforpheus.com. Starts uptown*

Be sure to bring a costume if you plan on visiting New Orleans for Mardi Gras.

at Napoleon Ave. and Tchoupitoulas St. and ends downtown at the Convention Center. *Lundi Gras (Mon). Begins 6pm.*

Mardi Gras Day Parades

❸ ★★★ **Zulu.** The premier African-American parade was originally created to parody haughty, race-restricted Rex. Now desegregated (both krewes welcome all members), Zulu riders still wear ironic attire like blackface and grass skirts. As the 35 floats and 1,200 riders pass, look for the famed Witch Doctor and Big Shot floats, and especially the prized Zulu coconuts: hand-painted souvenirs that even the natives scramble for. Hang out near the cops keeping the crowds in check; Zulu members typically pass coconuts to them as thanks. *www.kreweofzulu.com. Starts uptown at Jackson and Claiborne aves. and ends at Orleans Ave. and N. Broad St. Mardi Gras (Tues). Begins 8am.*

❹ ★★★ **Society of St. Anne.** Across town in the Bywater neighborhood, the bohemian Society of St. Anne musters around 10am. This fantastical walking club (no floats) is known for its madcap, au courant, sometimes risqué costumes and always wildly creative revelers. Due to overlapping timing, you'll have to make the tough choice between seeing this group and the Zulu parade. *Starts at Piety and Burgundy sts. Follows an unspecified route through Marigny and French Quarter, usually along Royal St. Ends at Canal St. Begins approx. 10am.*

❺ ★★ **Rex.** The King of Rex is also the King of Carnival, so this—the oldest parade (it debuted in 1872)—is the big kahuna. The royal costumes are a sight to behold—lots of glittery gold (and purple and

Prepping for Parade Mania

Arthur Hardy's *Mardi Gras Guide* is the unofficial Mardi Gras bible, from Twelfth Night (Jan 6, the official start of the Carnival season) through fat Tuesday, it covers the all-important parade schedule and includes a calendar of related events and informative articles on Carnival history. It's available all over the city—in bookstores, souvenir stores, groceries. You can also order an advance copy at www.arthurhardy.com and download the app, which includes the very useful parade tracker.

Begetting Beads

Want plenty of parade throws? On Mardi Gras day, "masking" (coming in costume) is essential. Definitely participate in some way, whether simple or outrageous. Yell the traditional phrase, "Throw me something, mister!" to show some Mardi Gras spirit. (And no, you needn't—and shouldn't—show skin. Save that for Bourbon Street, which doesn't have parades.) Bring a bag to haul your loot bead lust is contagious—and share the bounty with neighbors—there's plenty, and it's part of the fun (well, nobody shares the highly coveted coconuts from Zulu or shoes from Muses). Bring some starter snacks and beverages to be safe, though vendors usually walk the parade routes, and toilet paper for the rare and well-trafficked portolets.

green—they created the time-honored color combo, after all). The throws are fairly traditional, but every float's is different. *www.rex organization.com. Starts uptown at S. Claiborne and Napoleon aves. and ends downtown at Canal and South Peter sts. Mardi Gras (Tues). Begins 10am.*

❻ ★ kids Between and After the Parades. Families and kids ride their self-decorated "truck floats" and toss out toys and trinkets; pro-level high school marching bands make a mighty, precision sound; elegant *flambeaux* (torch-bearers) harken back to days of pre-electricity; and themed walking clubs range from nice to naughty to nutty. Some parade watchers go home after the "official" end of Mardi Gras with the passing of Rex, but these are almost (or even more) popular, the "true" closing parades, and very worth hanging around for. *Elks and Crescent City truck parades start uptown at S. Claiborne and Napoleon aves. and end in Mid-City at Tulane Ave. and S. Robertson St. Follows Rex.*

A crowd pleading and competing for "throws" from a passing float.

Jazz History: Where the Greats Got Their Starts

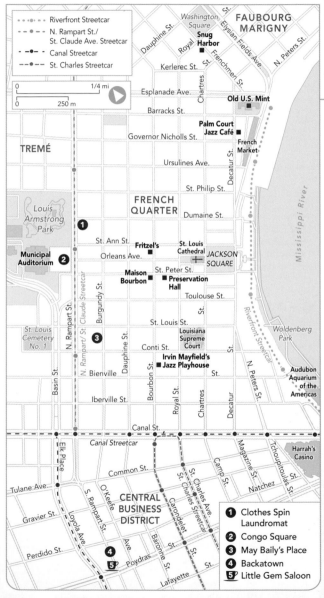

- ·····●····· Riverfront Streetcar
- - -●- - N. Rampart St./ St. Claude Ave. Streetcar
- -●- Canal Streetcar
- - -●- - St. Charles Streetcar

0 — 1/4 mi
0 — 250 m

FAUBOURG MARIGNY

Washington Square

Dauphine St.

Royal St.

Kerlerec St.

Frenchmen St.

N. Peters St.

Elysian Fields Ave.

Snug Harbor

Esplanade Ave.

Chartres St.

Old U.S. Mint

Barracks St.

Palm Court Jazz Café

Governor Nicholls St.

Decatur St.

French Market

TREMÉ

Ursulines Ave.

St. Philip St.

Louis Armstrong Park

FRENCH QUARTER

Dumaine St.

Mississippi River

1

St. Ann St.

Fritzel's

St. Louis Cathedral

JACKSON SQUARE

Municipal Auditorium

2

Orleans Ave.

Maison Bourbon

St. Peter St.

Preservation Hall

Toulouse St.

N. Rampart/ St. Claude Streetcar

Burgundy St.

Riverfront Streetcar

Woldenberg Park

St. Louis St.

St. Louis Cemetery No. 1

3

Dauphine St.

Louisiana Supreme Court

Conti St.

Bienville

Irvin Mayfield's Jazz Playhouse

N. Peters St.

Audubon Aquarium of the Americas

Basin St.

Bourbon St.

Iberville St.

Royal St.

Chartres

Decatur

Canal St.

Canal Streetcar

Harrah's Casino

Elk Place

Common St.

St. Charles Ave.

Magazine St.

Tchoupitoulas St.

Tulane Ave.

O'Keefe

St. Charles Streetcar

Camp St.

Natchez

Gravier St.

CENTRAL BUSINESS DISTRICT

Carondelet

S. Rampart St.

Loyola Ave.

Perdido St.

4

5

Baronne St.

Poydras St.

Lafayette

1 Clothes Spin Laundromat
2 Congo Square
3 May Baily's Place
4 Backatown
5 Little Gem Saloon

This tour visits key touchstones from the only true American musical form: jazz. When the cultural influences of two continents—Africa and Europe—collided in New Orleans, their energy and essences began to stew. Drums met horns and intertwined with keys and strings. When the rhythmic spice of the Caribbean and the emotions of societal circumstances were mixed in, a powerful musical brew began to bubble up. Add a dollop of time, a bit of brilliance, and something indefinable, and we got jazz. Amazingly, it all happened right here, along this path. START: **840 N. Rampart St.**

❶ ★ Clothes Spin Laundromat. Without jazz, there would be no rhythm and blues, no rock 'n' roll. This unassuming washeteria is surely the only laundromat that is also a Rock and Roll Hall of Fame landmark. It was the legendary recording studio of producer Cosimo Matassa, opening in 1945 as jazz was swinging and morphing into new musical forms. Arguably the first rock-and-roll record, Little Richard's "Tutti Frutti," was cut here, as were an astounding streak of influential hits by Fats Domino, Jerry Lee Lewis, Ray Charles, Irma Thomas, Sam Cooke, and gobs more. Check out the memorabilia displayed above the dryers in back. *840 N. Rampart St.*

Go 2 blocks south on Rampart Street to St. Peter Street.

❷ ★ Congo Square. This hallowed cultural ground (inside Armstrong Park in the Faubourg Tremé, the historic African-American neighborhood and "musical incubator"; see p 40) is widely recognized as the place where jazz began. Beginning in 1817, Napoleonic law (which still holds sway in Louisiana) and the Code Noir (Black Code) governing the treatment of slaves gave them Sundays off. They gathered here, creating a marketplace, a social scene, and a place to practice their Voodoo and Christian religions through prayer, drumming, chanting, and dancing. The movements, rhythms, and instruments of Africa joined those of the Creoles of Haiti, Spain, and France. These energetic festivities became more performance-oriented and eventually drew white onlookers and followers; it's said that madams from nearby brothels came to hire performers to entertain at their houses. As interest spread and the

Maison Bourbon.

sound transformed, new forms emerged, giving rise to jazz and a musical transformation that swept the world. *Inside Armstrong Park at N. Rampart and St. Peter sts.*

Walk uptown 1 block to Toulouse Street and turn left. Go 2 blocks and turn right at Dauphine Street.

❸ May Baily's Place & Storyville. This bar in the Dauphine Orleans Hotel is one of the few remnants of Storyville, the 16-block legalized red-light district based on and around nearby Basin Street. As the framed 1857 license hanging in the bar proves, May Baily's was a licensed house of ill repute (actually pre-dating Storyville, which thrived from 1898–1917). Hired musicians entertaining bordello guests helped to popularize jazz. The good times came to an abrupt end in 1917 when, at the Navy's behest, the city shut down Storyville "in an effort to curb vice because of the proximity of armed service personnel." But the swinging new sound was just beginning. *415 Dauphine St.*

Continue along Dauphine Street; turn right on Canal Street to

Harry Connick, Jr. and Branford Marsalis take the stage at Jazz Fest.

Rampart Street. (Note the fabulously renovated Saenger Theatre [see p 131], one of several old theaters recently renovated to all-new awesomeness.) Cross Canal Street and continue south along Rampart Street for 4 blocks.

❹ ★ Backatown. Serious jazz worshipers make a pilgrimage to this area, one of several called "Backatown" (from "back of town"). It's not much to look at besides boarded-up old buildings, yet it is perhaps the most significant block in American music history. The roots of jazz first grew out of Congo Square. But the Smithsonian considers the **Eagle Saloon** and third-floor **Odd Fellows Hall** (401 S. Rampart

Jazz Clubs

Jazz (and all its modern offspring) still thrives in New Orleans. Now that you've seen some touchstones, it's time to hear the real thing—and maybe shake a tail feather or cut a rug. Try one of these clubs (see also Chapter 7):

- **Fritzel's** (p 118), 733 Bourbon St.
- **Irvin Mayfield's Jazz Playhouse** (p 118), 300 Bourbon St.
- **Little Gem Saloon** (p 119), 445 S. Rampart St.
- **Old U.S. Mint** (p 51), 400 Esplanade Ave.
- **Palm Court Jazz Café** (p 119), 1204 Decatur St.
- **Preservation Hall** (p 119), 726 St. Peter St.
- **Snug Harbor** (p 118), 626 Frenchmen St.

Jazz Fest: *Laissez les bon temps roulez!*

What began in 1969 as a small gathering in Congo Square to celebrate the music of New Orleans has become a world-renowned phenomenon that ranks as one of the most respected, musically comprehensive events anywhere—and a heck of a good time. For two consecutive long weekends in late April and early May, New Orleans Jazz & Heritage Festival by Shell (the official name) turns the Fair Grounds Race Course into a mega-party. Nicknamed "Fest" or Jazz Fest, that hardly represents its scope, which spans alternative rock, Delta blues, hip hop, gospel, and Cajun folk (and yes, jazz in many forms) on 13 stages. Fest attracts superstars like Bruce Springsteen, Stevie Wonder, Lady Gaga, and Pearl Jam, yet the local and unknown acts are often the most rewarding. What elevates Fest is the "Heritage" part: It brings the NOLA. The food, art, and cultural exhibits are simply superb. If you come (and you should), book your hotel, flight, restaurant reservations, and nighttime show tickets early—months or up to a year out. That's before the bookings are announced, but the leap of faith will pay off. Info at New Orleans Jazz & Heritage Festival (1205 N. Rampart St.; ☎ 504/558-6100; www.nojazzfest.com).

St.) to be "The Birthplace of Jazz," for the pioneers who played here: greats like Buddy Bolden, Jelly Roll Morton, and King Oliver. Although dilapidated now, hopes run high to turn the Eagle Saloon into the New Orleans Music Hall of Fame. At the **Iroquois Theater** (413–415 S. Rampart St.), many musicians got their starts accompanying silent films and stage acts. A young Louis Armstrong

Little Gem Saloon.

won a talent contest there after buying his first cornet with money earned at the **Karnofsky Tailor Shop** (427–431 S. Rampart St.). The shop, now listed in the National Register of Historic Places, was owned by a white, Jewish family who raised and mentored a young Armstrong. *400 block of S. Rampart St*

5 ★★ **Little Gem Saloon.** Here at Frank Douroux's Little Gem Saloon, the Zulu Social Aid and Pleasure Club frequently started and ended its jazz funerals, and the greats also performed. After being shuttered and neglected for 40 years, the spiffed-up club re-opened in 2012, showcasing great live jazz in this area once again. Gulf oysters, cocktails, and Southern soul food should satisfy any hunger or thirst in your party. *445 S. Rampart St. www.littlegemsaloon. com.* ☎ 504/267-4863. *$$.*

The Best Museums

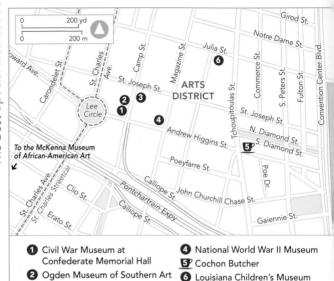

| 0 | 200 yd |
| 0 | 200 m |

1 Civil War Museum at Confederate Memorial Hall
2 Ogden Museum of Southern Art
3 Contemporary Arts Center
4 National World War II Museum
5 Cochon Butcher
6 Louisiana Children's Museum

Today's vibrant Arts District was once a shabby industrial collection of abandoned warehouses. Thanks to adaptive reuse, this once-rundown area has been transformed into a happening neighborhood, jammed with spacious museums showcasing Southern art, history, and heritage. The revitalization has spawned a fine gallery scene along Julia Street (stroll the 300–700 blocks), and given new life—and unified purpose—to an old neighborhood. START: **If you're in the Central Business District, it's an easy walk. Alternately, take the St. Charles streetcar to St. Joseph Street. Then walk east 2 blocks to Camp Street. Turn right and walk 1 block, past the Ogden Museum.**

1 ★★★ Civil War Museum at Confederate Memorial Hall. Here is the Confederate flag, that hot-button epicenter of controversy, displayed sans judgment. It's simply part of the second-largest collection of relics in the U.S., including documents, weapons,

uniforms, portraits, and the personal effects of Jefferson Davis and Robert E. Lee. The unusual 1891 pressed-brick Romanesque building is itself stunning, while an Alabama Legion battle flag with 83 painstakingly mended bullet holes is a moving reminder of this

A display of uniforms at the Civil War Museum at Confederate Memorial Hall Museum.

gruesome war. ⏱ 30–60 min. 929 Camp St. ☎ 504/523-4522. www. confederatemuseum.com. Admission $8 adults, $5 children 7–14, free for children 6 and under. Thurs–Sat 10am–4pm.

❷ ★★ **Ogden Museum of Southern Art.** In this dazzling modern building, galleries surrounding a soaring, glass-faced atrium house the premier collection of Southern art in the United States, by artists from 1890 to today. We particularly like the permanent exhibit of self-taught and outsider art, including some locals. If you go on a Thursday, **Ogden After Hours** presents live music in another gorgeous, wood-ceilinged anteroom. We're also keen on the well-curated gift shop, with its consistently covetable, artsy souvenirs. ⏱ 1–2 hr. 925 Camp St. ☎ 504/ 539-9650. www.ogdenmuseum.org. Admission $13.50 adults, $11 students/seniors, $7.25 children 5–17, free for children 4 and under. Wed–Mon 10am–5pm, live music Thurs 6–8pm.

❸ ★ **Contemporary Arts Center.** The CAC has three stories of airy galleries and (usually) a provocative, large-scale installation showing in the street-level windows. Modern art fans gather here for interesting, experimental, and sometimes influential work in various mediums, including theater, dance, music, and film. ⏱ 1 hr. 900 Camp St. ☎ 504/528-3800. www. cacno.org. Admission $10 adults, $8 college students/seniors; free to children and students through grade 12. Wed–Mon 11am–5pm.

Return south along Camp Street 1 block to Andrew Higgins Drive and turn left. Go 1 block to Magazine Street.

❹ ★★★ **National World War II Museum.** This must see, world-class facility boasts an abundant collection of artifacts, stellar videos, and plenty of advanced interactivity. Yet it still emphasizes the personal side of war, highlighted by veteran volunteers on site and

Live music is on hand at the Ogden's annual White Linen Night.

The National World War II Museum.

incredibly moving audio and video of civilians and soldiers recounting their first-hand experiences. Founded by the late historian and best-selling author Stephen Ambrose (author of *Band of Brothers* and a consultant to the film *Saving Private Ryan*), the museum now spans 6 acres and multiple themed buildings. Additionally, there are kicky, USO-style shows in the **BB's Stage Door Canteen;** a "4D" multisensory film, ***Beyond All Boundaries;*** and a pretty realistic mock submarine battle aboard **Final Mission: The USS Tang Experience.** ⏱ 2–3 hr. *945 Magazine St.* ☎ *504/527-6012 or 504/528-1944. www.nationalww2museum.org. Admission $24 adults, $20.50 seniors, $14.50 students/active military, free for children 4 and under and World War II veterans; separate admission for Beyond All Boundaries and Final Mission. Daily 9am–5pm. Closed holidays.*

Back on Andrew Higgins Drive, go east 2 blocks to Tchoupitoulas Street.

⑤ ★★★ **Cochon Butcher.** Squeamish, be warned: They do butcher hogs here. But excellent house-smoked meats and sausages will rock the carnivore's world. The pork belly sandwich with cucumber and mint is wondrous; the heated muffuletta rivals (maybe even bests?) more famous versions. Get the dreamy mac and cheese and swoonful caramel doberge cake too. *930 Tchoupitoulas St.* ☎ *504/588-7675. www.cochon butcher.com. $.*

A muffuletta at Cochon Butcher.

Mo' Museums

New Orleans's art scene—or scenes, more accurately—thrives well beyond the Arts District. There's great gallery browsing along all of **Royal Street** in the French Quarter and an edgy arts scene scattered along **St. Claude Avenue** (www.facebook.com/SCADNOLA). These museums, located elsewhere in the city, are also terrific:

- **Backstreet Cultural Museum** (p 42), 1116 Henriette Delille St.
- **Besthoff Sculpture Garden** (p 83), 1 Collins Diboll Circle.
- **McKenna Museum of African-American Art,** 2003 Carondelet St.
- **New Orleans Museum of Art** (p 14), 1 Collins Diboll Circle.
- **New Orleans Pharmacy Museum** (p 10), 514 Chartres St.
- **Southern Food & Beverage Museum,** 1504 Oretha Castle Haley Blvd.

Go north 2 blocks on Tchoupitoulas Street to Julia Street and turn left.

❻ ★★★ Louisiana Children's Museum. This fully interactive museum is more like a playground-meets-summer camp-meets-laboratory, in disguise. It'll keep kids occupied for a few hours. Along with changing exhibits, the museum offers art projects; all sorts of mini scenarios in which to play, shop, experiment, climb, and build;

a chance to "build" a New Orleans–style home; and lots of activities exploring music, fitness, science, and life itself. ⏱ 1½–2 hr. 420 Julia St. ☎ 504/523-1357. www.lcm.org. Admission $8.50, children under 1 free. Sept–May Tues–Sat 9:30am–4:30pm, Sun noon–4:30pm; June–Aug closing time is 5pm. Kids 15 and under must be accompanied by an adult. Closed major holidays.

Cooking demonstration at the Southern Food & Beverage Museum.

Faubourg Tremé

N. Claiborne Ave.

TREMÉ

FRENCH QUARTER

N. Rampart Street/St. Claude Avenue Streetcar

1 Congo Square
2 Armstrong Park
3 Candlelight Lounge
4 Lil' Dizzy's
5 New Orleans African American Museum of Art, Culture and History
6 Location from HBO's *Tremé*
7 St. Augustine Church
8 Backstreet Cultural Museum

Across Rampart Street from the French Quarter and a world away, the Faubourg Tremé was unusual from its 1730s inception. Claude Tremé, a Frenchman whose wife's family owned the land, began selling off lots to working-class Creoles and free people of color. Under French laws then governing Louisiana, they could own property. Thus, it is the country's oldest African-American community. It grew into a tight-knit, educated, and highly empowered community recognized for artistic progressiveness—not just in jazz and brass bands, as is well-known but also in fine arts, poetry, and literature. Recently popularized (and subsequently gentrified) thanks to HBO's post-Katrina series named for the area, the Tremé is a civil rights touchstone and still a massively influential and productive cultural incubator. Once considered unsafe for tourists, the Tremé is vastly improved. But crime persists, as in many parts of the city, so explore with a pal and heed your spidey sense. START: **Inside Armstrong Park at N. Rampart at St. Peter streets.**

1 ★★ **Congo Square.** This supremely significant corner of what is now Armstrong Park was

where African- and Haitian-born slaves and Creole free men of color were permitted to mingle, trade

Charles "Buddy" Bolden statue at Armstrong Park.

goods, worship, dance, drum, and create sounds that went on to give rise to a thing called jazz. *See p 33 Rampart and St. Peter sts, inside Armstrong Park.*

Walk through Armstrong Park toward the Mahalia Jackson Theater.

❷ ★ **Armstrong Park.** After families were displaced to clear the land for this park, it lay fallow for years. Later, the park was a haven for crime and drug users. It has finally emerged as a community point of pride, after extensive rehabbing, with activities, a sculpture garden, and the grand **Mahalia Jackson Theater.** *901 N. Rampart St. Park open daily 8am–6pm ('til 7pm during daylight savings).*

Walking tour of Armstrong Park.

Take the walkway to the right of Mahalia Jackson Theater, and exit the park onto St. Philip Street. Turn left, walk up St. Philip Street for 2 blocks, and go left on Robertson Street.

❸ ★★ **Candlelight Lounge.** Among the last of the great live music clubs—or perhaps the first of a new crop given the neighborhood's current energy. Wednesday nights when the Tremé Brass Band plays, it's the place to be. That's them on the mural. *925 North Robertson St.* ☎ *504/525-4748. Hours and cover charges vary. Tremé Brass Band plays most Wednesdays around 9:30pm, $10–$20 cover.*

Head back on Robertson Street, crossing St. Philip Street and continuing for 3 blocks to Esplanade Avenue.

❹ **Lil' Dizzy's.** This local diner is a gathering place for movers, shakers, neighbors, and nobodies, as much for the neighborhood lowdown as for the divine trout Baquet and stellar fried chicken. *1500 Esplanade Ave.* ☎ *504/569-8997. www.lildizzyscafe.net. Mon–Sat 7am–2pm; Sun 8am–2pm. $$.*

Take Esplanade Avenue 1 block south to Villere Street and turn right. Then take a left on Governor Nicholls Street.

Fountains at Mahalia Jackson Theater.

⑤ New Orleans African American Museum of Art, Culture and History. Although it is currently closed for renovations, this important center set in a lovely 1820s Creole villa is dedicated to protecting and promoting African-American history. We eagerly anticipate its reopening. *1418 Governor Nicholls St. www.noaam.org.*

Walk 1½ blocks down Governor Nicholls Street to Tremé Street and jog left.

⑥ Location from HBO's Tremé. The highly lauded HBO series *Tremé*, which ran from 2010 to 2014, went to great lengths to show the "real" New Orleans. It featured many local musicians, traditions, and locations, including this

Mardi Gras Indians at the Backstreet Museum.

one, home of D.J. Davis McAlary (played by Steve Zahn). *1212–1216 Tremé St.*

Head back to Governor Nicholls Street and turn left.

⑦ ★★ St. Augustine Church. Built in 1841 largely by blacks and free people of color, this was the first Catholic church to integrate African Americans and whites, at a time when they simply did not mix. After Katrina, the neighborhood and beyond successfully fought to save the church from closure by the Archdiocese. Don't miss the poignant Tomb of Unknown Slave (outside, facing Gov. Nicholls St.). The cross of chains draped with shackles honors slaves buried in unmarked graves. *1210 Gov. Nicholls St. (enter on Henriette Delille at Tremé St.). ☎ 504/525-5934. www.staugchurch. org. Sunday Jazz Mass 10am.*

From the front entrance to the church, cross Henriette Delille Street and turn right.

⑧ ★★★ Backstreet Cultural Museum. Owner Francis Sylvester displays his fascinating and essential collection of the cultural icons unique to this neighborhood: brass bands, jazz funerals, social aid and pleasure clubs, and especially Mardi Gras Indians. ⏱ *60 min. 1116 Henriette Delille St. ☎ 504/522-4806. www.backstreetmuseum.org. Admission $10. Tues–Sat 10am–4pm. ●*

The Upper French Quarter

1. Audubon Insectarium
2. Mississippi River
3. Aquarium of the Americas
4. Entergy Giant Screen Theatre
5. Woldenberg Park
6. Moon Walk
7. Crescent City Connection
8. Washington Artillery Park
9. Café du Monde
10. Pontalba Apartments
11. Jackson Square
12. The Presbytère
13. St. Louis Cathedral
14. The Cabildo
15. Le Petit Théâtre

The French Quarter—the heart of New Orleans—is positively packed with flavor, with something to stimulate every palate: from remarkable history to charming oddities, from high culture to low, boozy decadence. Founded in 1718, the Vieux Carré ("Old Square," its original name) comprised the original city of New Orleans. It burned twice—in 1788 and 1794—and rebuilding took place during Spanish rule, which explains why much of the architecture reflects a Spanish influence. Hotels, restaurants, and shops are now plentiful in this 6-by-13 block grid, but so are many historic sites, landmarks, and residences. This tour takes you to many of these old and new gems. The French Quarter is bordered by North Rampart Street, Esplanade Avenue, Canal Street, and the Mississippi River. START: **Canal Street, between Decatur and N. Peters streets.**

Previous page: Jackson Square.

❶ ★★★ kids **Audubon Insectarium.** Located in the former U.S. Customs House, this is the largest, free-standing museum in the world dedicated to its multi-legged and/or winged subjects. The journey through ickiness (Kidding! Bugs are fascinating!) covers 900,000 species. Even while dining at the **Tiny Termite Café,** you'll see silkworms spinning their fibers through glass-topped tables. It's a creepy, crawly, but peaceful departure from the hustle outside. ① *1–2 hr. 423 Canal St.* ☎ *504/524-2847. www.audubon institute.org/insectarium. Admission $20 adults, $15 seniors and children 2–12. Daily 10am–5pm.*

Head southeast on Canal Street toward the river, passing the aquarium and the Entergy Theater on your left.

❷ **Mississippi River.** Stroll along the parklike east bank of North America's second longest river and the reason for New Orleans's existence. At this point, the mighty waterway measures 1 mile (1.6km) across and 200 feet (60m) deep. *At the end of Canal St.*

Enjoying the exhibits at the Audubon Insectarium.

The Aquarium of the Americas is a great place to cool off and learn with the kids.

❸ ★★ kids **Aquarium of the Americas.** One of the top five aquariums in the country features an enormous tank with a see-through tunnel from which you can view sea creatures on all sides. There's a huge interior rain forest complete with birds, piranhas, and waterfalls, and plenty of touch-tank interactivity. You can peer down into a swamp and see Spots, a rare albino gator. The outdoor splash fountain might prove irresistible on a warm day. ① *1–2 hr. 1 Canal St.* ☎ *504/565-3033. www.audubon institute.org/aquarium. Admission $25 adults, $19 seniors and children 2–12. Daily 10am–5pm.*

❹ ★ kids **Entergy Giant Screen Theater.** The huge 3-D screen with all the A/V bells and whistles shows nature documentaries on everything from dinosaurs to the Rolling Stones. (Is that redundant?) ① *1–2 hr. Next door to the aquarium.* ☎ *504/581-4629. www.audubon institute.org. Tickets $12 adults, $10 seniors and children 2–12. Combo admissions available with other Audubon attractions. Daily 10am–5pm.*

Walk north through Woldenberg Park, along the Moonwalk board-walk, or hop on the Riverfront Streetcar.

Looking over the Mississippi from the Washington Artillery Park.

⑤ Woldenberg Park. Promenade along 20 acres (8 hectares) of open space along the riverfront with green lawns and public art, including an elegant Holocaust Memorial designed by Israeli artist Yaacov Agam, a pioneer of kinetic art. *Along the Mississippi River, btw. Iberville and Toulouse sts.*

⑥ ★★★ Moon Walk. This scenic brick and wood pathway is named for former New Orleans mayor and political scion Maurice Edwin "Moon" Landrieu. Built in the 1970s, it encouraged the public use and appreciation for the riverfront after preservationists struck down a proposal for an expressway along the river. At one point, the promenade's steps allow you to get right down to Old Muddy, and there are benches from which to view the city's busy port while enjoying a moonrise (or a muffuletta). *Along the Mississippi River, btw. Iberville and St. Philip sts.*

⑦ Crescent City Connection. The busy bridge comprises two separate steel spans, one completed in 1958, the second in 1988. It ranks as the fifth most traveled toll bridge in the country, with an annual traffic volume of more than 63 million vehicles. Spans the Mississippi River to Algiers Point.

⑧ Washington Artillery Park. From this platform, you get postcard-perfect views and selfie backgrounds of Ol' Man River or Jackson Square depending on which direction you face. Sit on the amphitheater steps for mule- and people-watching. *On Decatur St. next to Café du Monde.*

⑨ ★★★ kids Café du Monde. New Orleans's favorite coffeehouse, around since 1862, is known worldwide for its divine, powdered sugar–laden beignets and café au lait. Go off-hours to avoid the lines (late at night is best; breakfast is worst). *800 Decatur St.* ☎ *504/525-4544. www.cafedumonde.com. $.*

Cross Decatur St. to Jackson Square.

⑩ ★ Pontalba Buildings. Despite a shooting attempt on her life by her father-in-law and the acrimonious divorce that followed, heiress and Baroness Micaela Almonester de Pontalba became a savvy businesswoman and designed and built these exclusive town homes alongside Jackson Square in the 1840s (the largest private buildings in the country at the time). The ornamental cast ironwork (with her entwined initials,

"A.P.," in the design) inspired a now-familiar architectural trend. After the Civil War, respectable tenants began to move out; by 1900, the homes had fallen into slum-like conditions. Today, they're back to their original grandeur and highly coveted. The Louisiana State Museum maintains one, the 1850 House, that is open for tours. ① *30 min. 523 St. Ann St.* ☎ *504/524-9118. www.louisianastatemuseum.org/museums/1850-house. Admission $3 adults, $2 students, seniors, active military; free children 12 and under. Tues–Sun 10am–4:30pm.*

⓫ ★★★ **Jackson Square.** Once the site of public hangings and the gathering place for artillery, it's now the site of public events and a gathering place for visitors, street artists, and fortune tellers. This public space, named for Andrew Jackson after his victory in the 1815 Battle of New Orleans (that's him in the central sculpture, tipping his hat atop his steed) was built by Madame Pontalba, who modeled the classic layout after the Place des Vosges in Paris. *St. Ann and St. Peter sts. facing Jackson Square.*

⓬ ★★ **The Presbytère.** This, the Cabildo, and the St. Louis Cathedral—all designed by Gilberto Guillemard—were the first major public buildings in the Louisiana Territory. The Presbytère was built to house clergy serving in the cathedral. Spanish philanthropist and nobleman Don Andres Almonester y Roxas (Baroness Pontalba's father) financed the building, but he died in 1798, leaving only the first floor done. It was finally completed in 1813. Never used as a rectory, it became a city courthouse and now houses a Louisiana State Museum with excellent exhibits on Mardi Gras

and hurricanes. ① *60 min. 751 Chartres St.* ☎ *504/568-6968. www.louisianastatemuseum.org/museums/the-presbytere. Admission $6 adults, $5 students, seniors, active military; free children 12 and under. Tues–Sun 10am–4:30pm.*

⓭ ★★ **St. Louis Cathedral.** See p 9. *615 Pere Antoine Alley (on Jackson Square).*

⓮ ★★ **The Cabildo.** In the 1750s, this was the site of a French police station and guardhouse. Part of that building was incorporated into the Spanish government statehouse. It was still under reconstruction when the transfer papers for the Louisiana Purchase were signed in a room on the second floor in 1803. Since then, it has served as New Orleans's City Hall, the Louisiana State Supreme Court (the 1896 "separate but equal" *Plessy v. Ferguson* decision came down here), and, since 1911, a Louisiana history museum, famously housing Napoleon's death mask. Those old Civil War cannons out front? Not so obsolete. In 1921, in a near-deadly prank, one was loaded and fired. That missile traveled across the Mississippi, landing in a house in Algiers and narrowly missing its occupants. ① *60 min. 701 Chartres St.* ☎ *504/568-6968. www.louisianastatemuseum.org/museums/the-cabildo. Admission $6 adults, $5 students, seniors, active military; free children 12 and under. Tues–Sun 10am–4:30pm.*

⓯ ★ **Le Petit Théâtre.** This early-20th-century Spanish colonial–style building serves one of the oldest community theater troupes in the country and hosts the annual Tennessee Williams Literary Festival every spring. See p 130. *616 St. Peter St.* ☎ *504/522-2081. www.lepetittheatre.com.*

The Lower French Quarter

① 800–1000 blocks of Royal Street
  ①A Gallery Orange
  ①B Antieau Gallery
  ①C Red Truck Gallery
  ①D Tresor Gallery
② Madame John's Legacy
③ Miltenberger Houses
④ The Cornstalk Hotel
⑤ Café Amelie
⑥ Lafitte's Blacksmith Shop

⑦ The LaLaurie Mansion
⑧ Gallier Historic House Museum
⑨ Soniat House
⑩ Beauregard-Keyes House & Garden
⑪ Old Ursuline Convent
⑫ French Market
⑬ 521 Gov. Nicholls St.
⑭ Old U.S. Mint

The Lower Quarter is more residential and less touristy. "Upper" and "Lower" Quarter designations are used mostly by locals, but the distinction is clear. There are far fewer T-shirt and souvenir shops and many more condos, apartments, and single-family homes in this area, which will immerse you in history, charm you with unique architecture, and perhaps show its offbeat nature.
START: **Royal Street at St. Ann Street.**

① ★★★ 800–1000 blocks of Royal Street. For shopping rapture, walk any stretch of Royal Street. It's got street performers plus antiques, boutiques, all the

iques. Don't limit yourself to this stretch, but we do particularly love it for its slightly edgier art scene (sometimes called the "Low Road"), including **Gallery Orange** (819 Royal

St.), **Antieau Gallery** (927 Royal St.), **Red Truck Gallery** (938 Royal St.), and **Tresor Gallery** (1000 Royal St.).

While strolling Royal Street, detour right on Dumaine Street.

❷ ★ **Madame John's Legacy.** Dating to 1726, this building survived the great 1788 and 1794 fires that destroyed much of the French Quarter. Well, a few bits survived; the rest is rebuilt. Of the some 21 known owners and renters (including the son of the state's first governor), none were named John, or even Madame! Its moniker comes from a character in a George Washington Cable story. A rare example of the original French "raised cottage" architectural style, it now houses art exhibits as part of the Louisiana State Museum complex. ⏱ 60 min. 623 Dumaine St. ☎ 504/568-6968. www.louisianastate museum.org/museums/madame-johns-legacy. Free admission. Tues–Sun 10am–4:30pm.

Walk back to Royal Street and turn right.

❸ ★ **Miltenberger Houses.** It wasn't unusual for wealthy families to build homes for their offspring. But it's impressive that in 1838,

Cornstalk Hotel fence gate.

widow and single mother Aimée Miltenberger constructed residences for each of her three sons, at the then-lavish cost of $29,176. The walls are imported red-brick, and the design—while mostly Creole—shows some Greek revival influence. Note the oak leaves with acorns in the cast-iron details, a symbol of food, shelter, health, and hospitality. *900, 906 & 910 Royal St.*

❹ **The Cornstalk Hotel.** Legend persists that the fence surrounding this sweet Victorian was ordered by the home's owner to ease his wife's homesickness for her native Iowa. Oddly, the same story is told about a similar house and fence in the Garden District. Both were built by a Philadelphia foundry. Bill and Hillary Clinton and Elvis himself have walked the supposedly haunted halls here. *915 Royal St.*

A Miltenberger house.

🍴 ★★★ **Café Amelie.** The pretty-as-a-present courtyard and fresh, straightforward cafe cuisine are Amelie's calling cards, making it a lovely (and popular) lunch, brunch, or snack stop. (It's also where Beyoncé and Jay Z dined quite publicly after the scandalous Solange elevator episode.) If time is tight, offshoot Petite Amelie (a few doors down at 900 Royal St.; $) has tasty prepared grab-and-go options. *912 Royal St.* ☎ 504/412-8965. www.cafeamelie.com. $$.

From Royal and St. Philip streets, walk northwest 1 block to Bourbon Street.

6 ★★ Lafitte's Blacksmith Shop Bar. This National Historic Landmark claims to be the oldest continually operating bar in the country. Whether it was the headquarters of Jean Lafitte and his pirates—who posed as blacksmiths but fenced plundered goods here—remains legend; that this was one of Tennessee Williams's favorite watering holes is verified. An unfortunate exterior renovation, which attempts to give glimpses of the original brick-between-post construction method, makes it look fake (though it's not). ⏱ *30 min. 941 Bourbon St.* ☎ *504/593-9761. www.lafittesblacksmithshop.com. Daily 10am–3am.*

Go northeast on Bourbon Street to Gov. Nicholls Street and turn right to head back to Royal Street.

7 ★ The LaLaurie Mansion. Socialite Delphine LaLaurie and her physician husband were beloved for their extravagant parties, so when a slave girl fell from her roof under mysterious circumstances, neighbors chose to mind their own business. When a fire broke out here in 1834, Madame LaLaurie's gruesome, torturous treatment of her servants was exposed. Shocked neighbors ran her out of town. Now swanky condos, the property is said to be actively haunted. *1140 Royal St.*

8 ★ The Gallier Historic House Museum. The guided tour of this 1857 manse gives insight into mid-19th-century life in New Orleans and owner James Gallier's forward-thinking designs. The prominent and prolific local architect added unusual modern conveniences such as hot and cold running water, an indoor bathroom, and an indoor kitchen. ⏱ *45 min. 1132 Royal St.* ☎ *504/525-5661. www.hgghh.org. Admission $15 adults; $12 seniors, students & kids; free for children 7 and under and active military. Tours Mon, Tues, Thurs, and Fri at 10am, 11am, noon, 1pm, and 2pm; Sat at noon, 1pm, 2pm, and 3pm. Closed Wednesdays and Sundays.*

Head back to Gov. Nicholls Street and turn right. Turn right on Chartres Street.

9 ★★ Beauregard-Keyes House & Garden. This "raised cottage" with the handsome Doric columns was built in 1826 as a residence for wealthy New Orleans

The courtyard at the Beauregard-Keyes House.

auctioneer Joseph LeCarpentier. Confederate General P. G. T. Beauregard lived here between 1865 and 1867, as did author Frances Parkinson Keyes from 1944 until 1970. Her many novels about the region include *Dinner at Antoine's*, written here. The twin staircases, as one theory goes, provided separate arrival routes for men and women—denying men the chance of espying a lady's ankle. Another theory: they're awfully pretty. Mrs. Keyes's home, garden, and interesting collections of dolls and porcelain veilleuse teapots are open to the public. ⏱ *30 min. 1113 Chartres St. www.bkhouse.org.* ☎ *504/523-7257. Admission $10 adults; $9 seniors, students, and AAA members; $4 children 6–12; free for children 5 and under and active military. Mon–Sat 10am–3pm. Tours on the hour.*

⑩ ★ Old Ursuline Convent.

Built in 1752, this is the oldest building in the Mississippi River Valley. It was home to the hearty French nuns of Ursula, who provided the first decent medical care locally, saving countless lives; founded the first local school and orphanage for girls; and helped raise young French girls into marriageable prospects for the lonely men settling this territory. (Many locals claim to be direct descendants of those proper young girls—so many, in fact, that the math doesn't work.) It now houses 3 centuries of Catholic archives; historic religious icons; and supposedly, a ghost or two on the top floor. ⏱ *30 min. 1100 Chartres St.* ☎ *504/529-3040. www.stlouis cathedral.org/convent-museum. Admission $5 adults, $4 seniors, $3 students; children 6 and under free. Mon–Fri 10am–4pm; Sat 9am–3pm.*

Turn back toward Gov. Nicholls Street and turn right.

⑪ 521 Gov. Nicholls St. This

nearly 8,000-square-foot (743 sq. m), 1830s mansion served as Cosimo Matassa's recording studio in the 1950s. Musical legends of the time—including Fats Domino, Little Richard, Professor Longhair, and Allen Toussaint—recorded here. Some say it is haunted by the ghost of Professor Longhair; others look for a glimpse of Brad Pitt or Angelina Jolie, who purchased this stunning town home soon after Hurricane Katrina, bringing much-needed hope and awareness to the city (they've since sold). *521 Gov. Nicholls St. No public admission.*

Go northeast on Decatur Street to Esplanade Avenue.

⑫ ★★ Old U.S. Mint. This was

the site of Fort St. Charles, built to protect New Orleans in 1792. Andrew Jackson reviewed the "troops" here—pirates, ragtag volunteers, and a nucleus of actual trained soldiers—whom he later led in the Battle of New Orleans. It's the only building in America to have served as both a U.S. and a Confederate mint. It got pummeled during Katrina but now is a Louisiana State Museum housing coin and jazz collections (including Louis Armstrong's first trumpet). The third floor has a gorgeous performance space with entertainment most days, usually free (www.music atthemint.org). ⏱ *1–2 hr. 400 Esplanade Ave.* ☎ *504/568-6993. www. louisianastatemuseum.org/museums/ new-orleans-jazz-museum-the-old-us-mint. Free admission. Tues–Sun 10am–4:30pm.*

Garden District

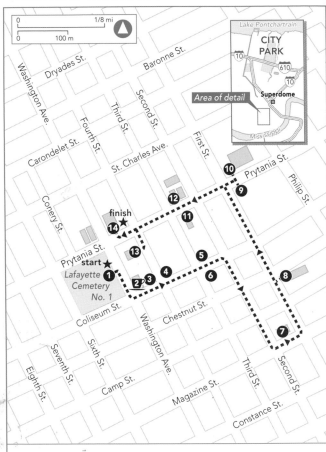

1. Lafayette Cemetery No. 1
2. Commander's Palace
3. Benjamin Button House
4. Koch-Mays House
5. Robinson House
6. Musson-Bell House
7. Payne-Strachan House
8. Rosegate
9. Toby's Corner
10. Bradish Johnson House
11. Davis House
12. Our Lady of Perpetual Help Chapel
13. Colonel Short's Villa
14. The Rink

fter the **1803 Louisiana Purchase**, the **Garden District** grew into a fashionable residential area for the *nouveau riche Americains*, who were not welcome among the French Quarter's wealthy, established Creole families. The culture clash is reflected through architecture. The lucrative combination of Mississippi River commerce, abundant slave trade, and national banks fueled the local economy, resulting in the remarkable antebellum building boom still on display in the many magnificent mansions and manicured gardens. Our favorite way to experience this exclusive neighborhood is to start with a tour of Lafayette Cemetery, followed by lunch at Commander's Palace, and then our walking tour. START: **1400 block of Washington Avenue.**

❶ ★★★ Lafayette Cemetery No. 1. Note the nameplates with Civil War battleground locales as the place of death in this 1833 burial ground, as well as many short-lived young people who likely perished in one of the city's yellow fever epidemics. See p 17. *1400 block of Washington Ave.*

❷ ★★★ Commander's Palace. If you're going to eat at one New Orleans restaurant, it should be Commander's Palace. Established in 1883 by Emile Commander, this turreted Victorian structure (a bordello back in the 1920s) has long reigned as one of the city's—nay, the country's—top restaurants. See p 100. *1403 Washington Ave.* ☎ 504/899-8221. www.commanderspalace.com. $$$.

From Commander's Palace, head east on Coliseum Street.

❸ ★ Benjamin Button House. This 8,000-square-foot (743 sq. m) site is best known as the title character's home in the film, *The Curious Case of Benjamin Button.* Ergo Brad Pitt slept here, fictionally. It's actually two houses: The original 1832 cottage was raised atop the columned, colonial number built in 1908. *2707 Coliseum St.*

The renowned Commander's Palace

❹ ★★ Koch-Mays House. This picturesque chalet-style dollhouse was built in 1876 by noted architect William Freret for James Eustis, a U.S. senator and ambassador to France (perhaps justifying the full-size ballroom). It and four other spec homes he built on the block were referred to as Freret's Folly. No detail was left unfrilled, from the ironwork to the gables and finials. *2627 Coliseum St.*

Continue east on Coliseum Street and turn left on Third Street.

❺ ★ Robinson House. This massive Italianate villa with the unusual curved portico took

Benjamin Button house.

architect Henry Howard 6 years to build (for tobacco grower Walter Robinson). The roof was designed to collect rainwater, thus pioneering indoor plumbing here. The lavish interior features a dining table seating 26 guests and a grand, curving staircase with 28 stairs. Amazingly, in post-depression times it sold for just $500. *1415 Third St.*

Walk south along Third Street and cross back over Coliseum Street.

Cast-iron balcony at the Robinson house.

6 ★ Musson-Bell House.
Edgar Degas's French Creole uncle, Michel Musson, was one of the few non-Americans to live in this nouveau riche neighborhood. Degas lived here too in another family home on Esplanade. Note the foundation of a once-common water tank on the Coliseum Street side: Mark Twain once commented that it looked as if everybody in the neighborhood had a private brewery. Most were destroyed when it was discovered that they bred disease-carrying mosquitos. *1331 Third St.*

Continue 2 blocks on Third Street and turn left on Camp Street. Go 2 blocks to First Street.

7 ★★ Payne-Strachan House.
Built in 1849, this antebellum Greek Revival home is best known as the place where Jefferson Davis, president of the Confederacy, passed away in 1889 while visiting friends. The sky-blue ceiling of the gallery, commonly seen around town, is believed to keep winged insects from nesting there and to ward off evil spirits. *1134 First St.*

Walk 1 block north on First Street.

8 ★★ Rosegate. Anne Rice's former home, the first to be built

Shops at The Rink.

on the block, in 1856, served as the setting for her Witching Hour series. Goth kids hung out here, waiting for a glimpse of their horror novelist hero. The delicate woven diamond and rosette pattern in the fence, which gave the Greek Revival town house its name, is said to be the precursor to the chain-link fence. *1239 First St.*

Continue up First Street 2 blocks and turn right on Prytania Street.

9 ★★ **Toby's Corner.** Philadelphian Thomas Toby's Greek Revival-style cottage melds Northern traditions with the practical applications of local Creole architecture, such as being raised on brick piers for increased cooling. Built in 1838, this is the oldest house in the Garden District. It changed hands in 1858 to a family whose descendants still live there. *2340 Prytania St.*

10 ★★ **Bradish Johnson House.** Sugar baron Bradish Johnson's ornate 1872 mansion cost an outlandish $100,000. Local architect James Freret's Parisian education and classical influences are evident in this stunning French-Second-Empire home, now part of the Louise S. McGehee School for Girls. Its awesome architectural detail—contrasted with the stark classical simplicity of Toby's Corner across the street—illustrates the effect of one

Bradish Johnson house.

generation of outrageous fortune. *2343 Prytania St.*

Head west on Prytania Street to the corner of Second Street.

11 ★★ **Davis House.** This gorgeous 1858 home belongs to the Women's Guild of the New Orleans Opera Association. It's one of the few area mansions available for tours and events. *2504 Prytania St.*

12 ★★ **Our Lady of Perpetual Help Chapel.** Originally built in 1858 as a private residence for wealthy merchant Henry Lonsdale, the home eventually served as a public chapel and was later owned by actor Nicolas Cage. *2521 Prytania St.*

Continue west on Prytania Street to Fourth Street.

13 ★ **Colonel Short's Villa.** The story goes that Short's wife missed the cornfields in her native Iowa, so he surrounded their 1859 Italianate manse with this unusual, cast-iron cornstalk fence. A revised explanation has the wife requesting it because it was the most expensive, showy fence in the building catalog. *1448 Fourth St.*

Cross Prytania Street.

14 ★ **The Rink.** Originally a roller-skating rink built in 1884 and later a mortuary, this quaint shopping center serves up a coffee shop, bookstore, boutiques—and restrooms. *2727 Prytania St.* ☎ *504/899-0335.*

Bayou St. John

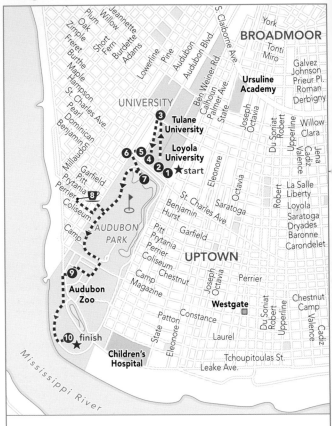

1 Loyola University
2 Holy Name of Jesus Church
3 Tulane University
4 Gibson Hall
5 Zemurray Mansion
6 Park View Guest House
7 Audubon Park
8 Tartine
9 Audubon Zoo
10 The Fly

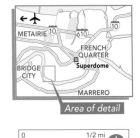

0   1/2 mi
0   0.5 km

Once a busy waterway used by Native Americans, Bayou St. John now offers a sleepy respite from urban life. You may either follow the sidewalk for a close-up view of the cottages, shotgun houses (a house laid out in such a straight line that you could shoot a shotgun through the front door and the ammo would go straight out the back door), and Greek Revival homes, or scramble down the small grassy levee to the edge of the water and look for fish, turtles, frogs, and ducks. When you cross Grand Route St. John, you're standing on the oldest street in New Orleans, originally a Native American portage between the bayou and the Mississippi River. In 1699, the Biloxi Indians guided French Louisiana colonists and brothers Pierre Le Moyne d'Iberville and Jean-Baptiste Le Moyne de Bienville through what is now Grand Route St. John. START: **Hagan Avenue and Toulouse Street.**

1 ★★★ **Parkway Bakery.** If it's not quite po'boy hour yet (isn't it always?), get 'em to go and enjoy them along the bayou later on. If you get the roast beef, which you should, get lots of napkins. And some Zapp's chips. See p 106. *538 Hagan Ave.* ☎ *504/482-3047. $.*

Head up Toulouse Street to the Bayou.

2 **Remembering the Flood.** It's important, and still shocking, to note that post-Katrina there was 10 feet (3 m) of water in the street you've just crossed. Parkway, which flooded completely, re-opened barely 3 months after the storm; the Obama family noshed there on the flood's 5-year anniversary. *Bayou St. John at Toulouse St.*

Walk east along Bayou St. John, which parallels Moss St. Note that both sides of the Bayou are called Moss St. You'll stay on the same side.

3 **Louis Blanc House.** This is one of the oldest homes on the bayou (predating the 1803 Louisiana Purchase). Moss Street is named for the Spanish moss hanging from live oak trees bordering the bayou. *924 Moss St.*

4 **The Old Portage.** This historic landmark on the bayou side of the street marks the point at which ships from France, Spain, the West Indies, and elsewhere ended their journey. From here, the imported goods were carried (or "ported") over land or by a small canal to the French Quarter and environs. Commercial activity on the Bayou continued until 1936. *On the bayou side of the intersection of Moss and Bell sts.*

5 **Old Spanish Custom House.** Believed to be the oldest surviving residence in New Orleans, this elegant, West Indies–style plantation home was built in 1784. It probably served to collect tolls and jail smugglers when trading ships

Louis Blanc house.

The Old Spanish Custom House may be the oldest surviving residence in New Orleans.

plied this bayou. General Andrew Jackson met with the pirate Jean Lafitte here. The 3000-square-foot (278 sq. m) mansion was sold in 2009 for just over $1 million. *1300 Moss St. at Grand Route St. John.*

6 ★★ **Pitot House.** This house was built around 1799 for the first mayor of incorporated New Orleans. In 1962, a proposed expansion of Cabrini High School threatened its existence, so the Louisiana Landmarks Society moved the house here from a block

The wide galleries of the Pitot House are typical of West Indies–style architecture.

away. Now a museum, its wide galleries and large rounded columns are typical of a West Indies–style plantation home. ⏱ *45 min (for tour). 1440 Moss St. See p 14.*

7 **Cabrini High School.** Maria Francesca Cabrini started the first missionary order of women in 1881. She and the Italian sisters came to America to open schools, hospitals, and an orphanage on Esplanade (now a girls' high school). The extraordinary Mother Cabrini was inducted into the National Women's Hall of Fame and named the first American Citizen Saint, Patroness of Immigrants. *1400 Moss St. www.cabrinihigh.com.* ☎ *504/482-1193. Free admission. Tours by appointment only.*

8 ★ **Magnolia Bridge.** Thought to be the oldest bridge in the city, the circa 1880 steel "swing bridge" (it pivots out from the center point) was built for heavy traffic, including streetcars. It allowed boat passage until 1936. *Across from Cabrini High, 1400 Moss St., at Harding Dr.*

Cross Magnolia Bridge over the bayou and turn left to take in the historic homes along the west or

The Voodoo Queen of Bayou St. John

Voodoo in New Orleans is a unique combination of beliefs borrowed from African animism, Haitian spirits, and Roman Catholicism. The latter was likely incorporated to placate the local authorities. Even so, the city's European population feared voodoo and its practitioners (due to misrepresentations that persist today). In the late 18th century, Spanish Governor Galvez banned slaves from Martinique, believing that their devotion to voodoo made them dangerous. Police raids in the French Quarter drove voodoo practitioners out to the "country" along Bayou St. John. Priestess Marie Laveau (1801–1881), an influential free woman of color, made good use of her connections with servants throughout the city. She knew secrets about the elite that were attributed to black magic but were most likely due to spying, blackmail, and her career as a hairstylist to the wealthy. Nevertheless, she drew thousands of believers to the "Wishing Spot" on the bayou. They supposedly drank the blood of roosters and danced with snakes, the earthly symbol of the voodoo god. Legit Voodoo ceremonies are still held here, notably on St. John's Eve, each June 23rd on Magnolia Bridge.

"lake" side of Moss Street and Bayou St. John.

⑨ ★ Historic homes. Along this walk and the neighboring streets, you'll see many Creole cottage, colonial, Victorian, Greek Revival, and shotgun homes. The different styles serve as a veritable timeline of when they were built. As the city's drainage system improved, it allowed for more residential development. In its early

Magnolia Bridge.

days, working plantations and "country homes" for wealthy city folk were abundant here. *1300–900 blocks of West Moss St.*

At Dumaine Street, turn right and walk 5 blocks northwest to Carrollton Avenue.

⑩ ★★ Pandora's Snoballs. Choose your sweetness from 100+ flavors atop feather-light, shaved ice. For extra decadence, try it "stuffed" with soft-serve ice cream. Don't be discouraged by the mob or the wait; on a hot day there's nothing like it. ⏲ *30 min. 901 N. Carrollton Ave.,* ☎ *504/486-8644. $.*

To reach fabulous City Park (p 82), continue along Carrollton Avenue for 2 blocks. Or grab the streetcar back to your original destination.

Bywater & St. Claude Avenue

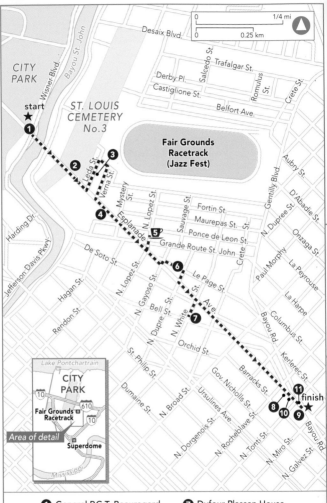

1 General P.G.T. Beauregard Equestrian Statue

2 St. Louis Cemetery No. 3

3 Luling Mansion

4 Terranova's Supermarket

5 Liuzza's by the Track

6 Cresson House

7 Dufour Plassan House

8 Reuther House

9 Tinted Town Homes

10 Degas House

11 Goddess of History– Genius of Peace Statue

This is a hearty walk (or a good bike ride) through an architecturally and demographically diverse—and diversifying—historic neighborhood (see p 165 for bike rentals). Originally home to landed French Creole gentry; then modest, working plantations; and later (and still) home to working-class manumitted slaves and Haitian, Irish, and German immigrants, it's now an artists' stronghold in a fascinating phase of degeneration meets regeneration. For decades, ships ported here and warehouses lined the river, bringing coffee, bananas, sugar, and cotton to and from New Orleans. At one time, the largest cotton press in the world was here, as was a major U.S. Navy installation until 2013. Nowadays, the indie/alternative nightclub scene along St. Claude is a draw every night. The second Saturday of each month (6–9pm) is a particularly good time to hit the avenue for the arts walk (www.secondsaturdaystclaude.com), when the friendly laid-back vibe is punctuated with the energy of a burgeoning arts movement. Use caution in this transitioning area, especially after dark. START: **St. Claude Avenue at Spain Street.**

① ★ Barrister's Gallery. The always-interesting ethnographic and contemporary outsider art featured here is some of the best of the eclectic St. Claude Avenue arts scene. ① 15 min. 2331 St Claude Ave. ☎ 504/710-4506. www.barristersgallery.com. Tues–Sat 11am–5pm.

②P ★★ St. Roch Market. At once a stunning restoration of the historic center of this working-class neighborhood and a glaring symbol of its recent gentrification, the food hall showcases 15 varied vendors with something to please every palate. ① 30 min. 2381 St. Claude Ave. ☎ 504/609-3813. www.strochmarket.com. $.

St. Roch Market.

The Steamcog Dixieland band at Marigny Opera House.

Cross St. Claude Avenue and head South on St. Roch Street for 3 blocks. At Dauphine Street, turn left. Walk another 3 blocks to St. Ferdinand Street and turn right.

③ **Marigny Opera House.** In its day (built in 1847), this elaborate church served the area's German Catholics. Now, the "church of the arts" presents an eclectic array of theater, dance, cultural, and community events, including its own ballet company. If it's open, step inside to check out the stained glass (and admire the new owners' in-process restoration ambitions). *725 St. Ferdinand St.* ☎ *504/948-9998. www.marignyoperahouse.org.*

Continue down St. Ferdinand Street and turn left at Royal Street.

④ **Homer Plessy marker.** On this site in 1892, Homer Plessy was arrested after intentionally boarding a whites-only train, leading to the *Plessy vs. Ferguson* "separate but equal" Supreme Court decision that institutionalized segregation laws until overturned in *Brown vs. Board of Education* (1954). In 2009, descendants from both sides of that trial united at the installation of this marker. *Corner of Royal & Press sts.*

Turn right onto Press Street and continue to Chartres Street.

⑤ **New Orleans Center for Creative Arts.** This impressive facility is a leading-edge arts school whose famous alumni include Harry Connick Jr., Terence Blanchard, the Marsalis brothers, Wendell Pierce and Trombone Shorty. *2800 Chartres St.* ☎ *504/940-2850. www. nocca.com.*

At Chartres Street, make a left. The changes to this neighborhood are evident in the contrast between the renovated restaurants and condos in the Rice Mill Lofts on the right and the standard working warehouse sheds on the left.

⑥ ★★★ **Dr. Bob's Studio.** Home to the ubiquitous, bottle-cap-studded "Be Nice or Leave" sign, and much more expansive, impressive artworks. Fun Bywater fact: Arguably the first modern boxing match in the U.S. was fought here in 1892, when "Gentleman" Jim Corbett knocked out John Sullivan in the 21st round. The arena was thought to be on the site where Dr. Bob's studio now stands. ⏱ *45 min. 3027 Chartres St.* ☎ *504/945-2225. www.drbobart. net. Open "by chance or appointment" (we've had good luck).*

Continue 2 blocks along Chartres Street.

7 ★★ Piety Bridge and Crescent Park. The elegant, severe archway (quickly dubbed the "Rusty Rainbow" by locals) leads to a picturesque new riverfront park. Stellar views provide Polaroid moments and a good perspective on the ports and warehouses of this working waterway. *Piety & Chartres sts. See p 89.*

At Piety Street., turn left and walk 3 blocks. You'll pass Pizza Delicious, a fine choice if you need refreshments. Turn left on Burgundy Street. Optionally, detour right 1 block to Desire Street, where a noted streetcar once ran. Take a photo under the street sign, then double-back 2 blocks on Burgundy.

8 ★★★ Christopher Porché West Gallery. We fervently aspire to own one of Porché West's haunting photographs set in intricate architectural assemblages. ⏱ *30 min. 3201 Burgundy St.* ☎ *504/947-3880. www.porche-west.com. Irregular daytime hours. If it looks closed, knock anyway.*

And now for your food and drink stop: Turn left on Louisa Street and walk 1 block to Dauphine Street.

9 ★★★ Oxalis. Cool down at this ultrasmart gastropub with a warren of rooms (a cool and comfy main room, sultry patio, and hipster back bar) and a booze selection on steroids, ranging from tippy-top shelf to "plastic cap." The tasty, globally inflected menu features sweet potato poutine, mussels in tangy coconut milk, and crispy, sticky, Korean-style wings. *3162 Dauphine St. www.oxalisbywater. com.* ☎ *504/267-4776. $$.*

Last stop, if you can make it, is a noted local church. Hearty walkers head back from here; others will want to taxi back to their origins.

10 Blessed Francis Seelos Xavier Church. The towering brick building with the vaulted ceiling and beautiful stained glass has served the deaf community since the 1860s. Hearing and non-hearing people from all over came to participate in its post-Katrina renovation. *3053 Dauphine St. www. seeloschurchno.org.* ☎ *504/943-5566; TTY/voice 504/943-2456. Mon–Fri 8am–4pm; Sat noon–5pm; Sun mass 7:30am.*

Guitar Slim, Jr. at the blues workshop at New Orleans Center for Creative Arts.

Esplanade Ridge

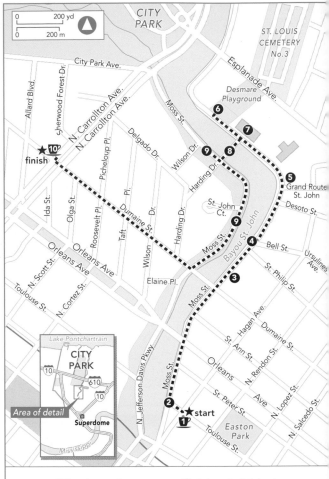

1. Parkway Bakery
2. Remembering the flood
3. Louis Blanc House
4. The Old Portage
5. Old Spanish Custom House
6. Pitot House
7. Cabrini High School
8. Magnolia Bridge
9. Historic homes
10. Pandora's Snoballs

On Esplanade Avenue, the sounds of city life are muffled by giant oak trees whose massive roots twist the sidewalks into roller coasters. The tweets and squawks of bird life add to the exotic atmosphere. In the spring, confederate jasmine perfumes the neighborhood. In the summer, delicate crape myrtles are in full bloom. Block after block of imposing historic homes—from Victorians to raised villas—remind us that this was the Creole elite's enclave in the late 1800s. The lots and lawns are not quite as expansive as those along St. Charles, and some homes have seen better days. Still, it's closer to the soul of the city than St. Charles Avenue (read: regular people live here, whereas St. Charles always was and still is for the well-heeled. START: **Esplanade Avenue at N. Carrollton Avenue, the entrance to City Park (end of the "City Park" spur off the Canal Street streetcar line).**

❶ General P.G.T. Beauregard Equestrian Statue. This 1915 statue of Civil War General Beauregard may not be here for long. It's among New Orleans's controversial historic monuments (along with statues of Robert E. Lee and Jefferson Davis) to Confederate "heroes," whom many believe should no longer hold prominent places of honor. *Traffic circle at Esplanade Ave. and N. Carrollton Ave., across from main entrance to City Park.*

Cross the bridge and Bayou St. John and continue down Esplanade Avenue.

❷ ★★★ St. Louis Cemetery No. 3. Home to wealthy Creole families from 1835 on, it contains the burial monuments of many of the local diocese's priests and religious orders. It might also be called "Restaurateurs' Rest": The tombs for the Galatoire, Tujague, and Prudhomme families are here. It remains active, safe, and well cared for. See p 13. *3421 Esplanade Ave.*

Turn left at the brick-columned entrance to Leda Court.

❸ ★ Luling Mansion. Originally, this private residence of sugar and cotton baron Florence Luling had a

The P.G.T. Beauregard equestrian statue.

full moat and 80 acres of land (look for the cursive "L" on the concrete fenceposts at Esplanade Avenue). In 1871 it became the Jockey Club for the new Fair Grounds racetrack. Although unfortunate modern adjustments have taken a toll, its original Italianate magnificence is still apparent. *1436 Leda Court.*

Return to Esplanade Avenue.

❹ ★ Terranova's Supermarket. As you explore the city, note the houses with front doors oriented toward a street corner. Many were

Luling Mansion.

once family-run corner groceries like this, which is run by the third generation of Terranovas (and still making tasty sausage). *3308 Esplanade Ave.* ☎ *504/482-4131. Mon–Fri 8am–6:30pm, Sat 9am–6:30pm; closed Sun.*

Slight left onto Ponce de Leon Street. Note the charming pocket park on Esplanade, and the cluster of small shops and restaurants here. These are emblematic of New Orleans's many charming neighborhoods.

☕ ★★★ **Liuzza's by the Track.** There's a story (or three) on every barstool here, and many more behind the bar. But you're here for the gumbo and a shrimp or oyster po'boy (or both). Others opt for the portabella salad. Chat with the locals and cool down with a big schooner of brew or a sweet tea. See p 105. *1518 N. Lopez St. $.*

From here, peer down N. Lopez Street to espy the Fair Grounds Race Course, one of the oldest racetracks in the country (founded in 1872). Attending on Opening Day (a.k.a. Thanksgiving) is a local tradition. The world-famous New Orleans Jazz & Heritage Festival is also held here. Explore it if you prefer, or turn right on N. Lopez and head back to Esplanade Avenue and head left.

❻ **Cresson House.** This uniquely decorative, turreted Queen Anne, built in 1902, is frilly even by New Orleans standards. Note the dainty fleur-de-lis design on the heavy cast-iron gate. *2809 Esplanade Ave.*

Turn right on the next block, N. White Street.

❼ **Dufour Plassan House.** This 1870 mansion, noted for its whimsically painted iron cornstalk-and-sunflower fence, is relatively young compared to its neighbors on the bayou. It was moved here from Esplanade in 1906. *1206 N. White St.*

New Orleans Jazz Festival at the Fair Grounds.

Degas house.

Double-back to Esplanade Avenue and turn right.

8 Reuther House. Check out the collection of metal and cinder-block sculptures in this front yard. The current residents are artists, co-founders of the Contemporary Arts Center and major figures in the city's arts community. Also note the neighboring homes at nos. 2325, 2327, 2329, and 2331—all are interesting examples of Creole cottages. *2326 Esplanade Ave.*

9 Tinted Town Homes. Originally built in 1883 as spec town homes, these three Candy Crush–colored Italianate houses now comprise La Belle Esplanade B&B. Try to look beyond the, um, vivid tones to note each home's architectural identity, including the intricate mill-work. *2212, 2216, 2222 Esplanade Ave.* ☎ *504/301-1424. www.labelle esplanade.com.*

10 ★ Degas House. The Musson family rented this 1854 house for many years. Estelle Musson married René Degas, brother of Edgar Degas, the French Impressionist

artist. (She and her descendants dropped the Degas name after René ran off with a neighbor's wife.) Edgar Degas lived here briefly and painted a portrait of Estelle that now hangs in the New Orleans Museum of Art. The split home now operates as a B&B, event venue, and museum (tours are offered) *2306 Esplanade Ave.* ☎ *504/821-5009. www.degashouse.com.*

11 Goddess of History— Genius of Peace Statue. In 1886, this triangular plot, called Gayarre Place, was given to the city by Charles Gayarre. George H. Dunbar donated the terra-cotta statue, a victory monument. It was destroyed in 1938 and replaced with the present cement and marble model. *Esplanade Ave. and N. Tonti St.*

One mile down Esplanade Avenue is Rampart Street, which borders the French Quarter. The #91 bus will take you there. Stay on it if you're returning to the Central Business District.

Uptown

start ❶
❷ St. Roch Market

Marais St.
St. Claude Ave.
Elysian Fields Ave.
N. Rampart St.
Spain St.
St. Roch Ave.
Music St.
Burgundy
Mandeville St.
Marigny St.

FAUBOURG MARIGNY

Washington Square

St. Ferdinand St.
Press St.
Port St.
Franklin Ave.
Chartres St.

Dauphine St. **finish** ❿
Royal St.
❸
❹
❺
❻

Clouet St.

Urquhart St.
Marais St.
St. Claude Ave.
Montegut St.
N. Rampart St.
Burgundy St. **BYWATER**

Louisa St.
Piety St.
❾ ❽
❼

Crescent Park

Mississippi River

- **❶** Barrister's Gallery
- **❷** St. Roch Market
- **❸** Marigny Opera House
- **❹** Homer Plessy marker
- **❺** New Orleans Center for Creative Arts
- **❻** Dr. Bob's Studio
- **❼** Piety Bridge and Crescent Park
- **❽** Christopher Porché West Gallery
- **❾** Oxalis
- **❿** Blessed Francis Seelos Xavier Church

- – • – N. Rampart Street/ St. Claude Ave. Streetcar

0 _____ 1/4 mi
0 _____ 0.25 km

Uptown is a "neighborhood" in all the traditional senses, where families, students, and young professionals are on a first-name basis with the mom-and-pop grocers down the block. It's also the largest neighborhood in the city (and those small biz grocers now compete with Whole Foods). Bounded by the Mississippi River and Carrollton, Claiborne and Jackson avenues (although anything west of the Pontchartrain Expressway is often referred to as "Uptown"), plush live oak tree branches overhang the historic homes, ranging from modest to mansion. The largely upscale area still feels modest and historic. START: **St. Charles Avenue and West Road (or take the St. Charles Streetcar to the Tulane/Loyola stop.**

❶ ★ **Loyola University.** Jesuits were early pioneers in shaping New Orleans's history, including introducing sugar cane to the region in the late 18th century. In 1849, they opened the College of the

Immaculate Conception downtown, and acquired the larger "suburban" tract of land across from Audubon Park for $22,500 in 1886. Loyola College opened its doors in 1906, and today serves over 4,600 students.

Loyola University.

6363 St. Charles Ave. ☎ 800/456-9652 or 504/865-3240. www.loyno.edu.

② ★ **Holy Name of Jesus Church.** In 1913, when the parish outgrew its little wooden chapel, construction began on this larger church thanks to a $150,000 donation. The large altar of carved Carrera marble cost $12,000. The tall bell tower is visible from the far reaches of Audubon Park. Although the church still has its original 1892 bell, an electric keyboard now chimes out. It also sounds lovely. 6367 St. Charles Ave. ☎ 504/865-7430. www.hnjchurch.org.

③ ★★ **Tulane University.** Founded by seven doctors in 1834 as the Medical College of Louisiana, it became the esteemed Tulane University of Louisiana in 1884 after Paul Tulane donated $1 million. More than 13,000 students

attend the private, nonsectarian research university, which has been at this location since 1894, and is the largest private employer in New Orleans. 6823 St. Charles Ave. ☎ 504/865-5000. www.tulane.edu.

④ ★ **Gibson Hall.** This massive neo-Romanesque building was built in 1894, the first to be constructed on the current Uptown Tulane campus. 6823 St. Charles Ave. ☎ 504/865-5000. www.tulane.edu.

⑤ ★ **Zemurray Mansion.** This formidable 1908 Greek revival mansion was owned for years by Russian-born Samuel "Sam the Banana Man" Zemurray, a massively successful fruit and produce importer whose global influence was tied to revolutions in Honduras and Guatemala. His young niece, author Lillian Hellman, played here as a child. After his death in 1961, his widow bequeathed the mansion to Tulane University. It has served as

The Greek revival–style columns of the Zemurray Mansion.

Picnic at The Fly.

the Tulane president's residence ever since. *7000 St. Charles Ave.*

6 Park View Guest House. This popular bed-and-breakfast was built as a boarding house in the late 1800s and is listed on the National Register of Historic Places. *7004 St. Charles Ave.* ☎ *888/533-0746 or 504/861-7564. www.parkviewguesthouse.com.*

7 ★★ kids Audubon Park. See p 90. *6500 St. Charles Ave. (across from Tulane and Loyola universities, btw. St. Charles Ave. & Magazine St.).* ☎ *504/581-4629.*

8 ★★ Tartine. Midway through the park, detour through the neighborhood along the uptown side to this charming French cafe for excellent sandwiches, generous salads

(including a perfect Nicoise), and yummy pastries. Also the best bagels in town, baked in house. Get it to go to eat at The Fly (see below). *7217 Perrier St.* ☎ *504/866-4860. $.*

9 ★★★ kids Audubon Zoo. See p 91. ⏱ *2–3 hr. 6500 Magazine St.*

10 ★★ kids The Fly. Follow the curved road to the right of the zoo and you'll come to this popular riverside park, nicknamed "The Fly" because the land is shaped like a butterfly. It's fun to watch passing ships, tugboats, and tankers. Bring a picnic, find a Frisbee, and make like a local. *Riverview Dr. off Magazine St. btw. Audubon Zoo and the Mississippi River.* ●

Shopping Best Bets

Best **T-Shirt Designs**
★★ Dirty Coast, *5631 Magazine St. and 2121 Chartres St. (p 76)*

Best **Shoe Store**
★★ Feet First, *4122 Magazine St. and 526 Royal St. (p 76)*

Best **Hatter**
★★★ Meyer the Hatter, *120 St. Charles Ave. (p 77)*

Best **Record Store**
★★★ Domino Sound, *2557 Bayou Rd. (p 80)*

Best **Record Store for Local Music**
★★★ Louisiana Music Factory, *421 Frenchmen St. (p 80)*

Best **Record Store for Vinyl**
★★ Euclid Records, *3301 Chartres St. (p 80)*

Best **Used Bookstore**
★★ Crescent City Books, *124 Baronne St. (p 76)*

Best **New Bookstore**
★★★ Faulkner House, *624 Pirate's Alley (p 76)*

Best **Men's Grooming Products (and Shave)**
★★★ Aidan Gill, *550 Fulton St. and 2026 Magazine St. (p 75)*

Best **Photography Gallery**
★★★ A Gallery for Fine Photography, *241 Chartres St. (p 78)*

Best **Art Gallery**
★★★ Antieau Gallery, *927 Royal St. (p 78)*

Best **Vintage Women's Wear**
★★ Lili Vintage, *3329 Magazine St. (p 77)*

Best **Vintage-Inspired Women's Wear**
★★★ Trashy Diva, *537 Royal St. and 2048 Magazine St. (p 77)*

Best **Classic Menswear Store**
★★ Rubenstein's, *102 St. Charles Ave. (p 77)*

Best **Outrageous Antiques Store**
★★★ M.S. Rau, *630 Royal St. (p 74)*

Best **Chocolates**
★★★ Sucre, *3025 Magazine St.; 622 Conti St. (p 78)*

Best **Pralines**
★★ Southern Candymakers, *334 and 1010 Decatur St. (p 78)*

Best **Secondhand Book Shop**
★★ Beckham's Bookshop, *228 Decatur St. (p 75)*

Previous page: Jackets and dresses at Muse.

Royal Street Shopping

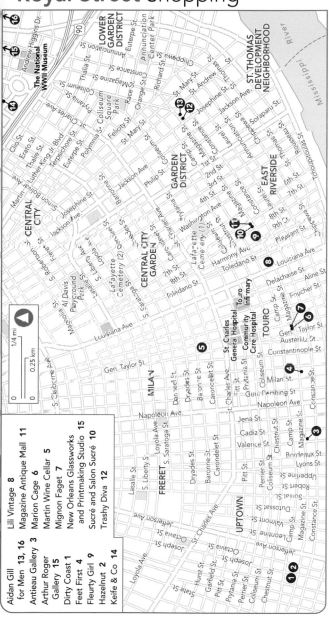

Aidan Gill
for Men **13, 16**
Antieau Gallery **3**
Arthur Roger
Gallery **15**
Dirty Coast **1**
Feet First **4**
Fleurty Girl **9**
Hazelnut **2**

Lili Vintage **8**
Magazine Antique Mall **11**
Marion Cage **6**
Martin Wine Cellar **5**
Mignon Faget **7**
New Orleans Glassworks
and Printmaking Studio **15**
Sucré and Salon Sucré **10**
Trashy Diva **12**

Keife & Co **14**

Magazine Street Shopping

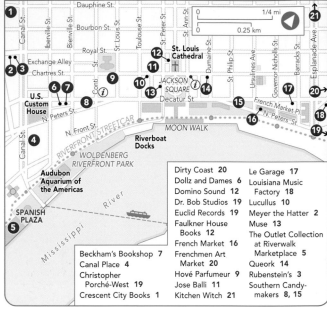

Beckham's Bookshop **7**
Canal Place **4**
Christopher Porché-West **19**
Crescent City Books **1**
Dirty Coast **20**
Dollz and Dames **6**
Domino Sound **12**
Dr. Bob Studios **19**
Euclid Records **19**
Faulkner House Books **12**
French Market **16**
Frenchmen Art Market **20**
Hové Parfumeur **9**
Jose Balli **11**
Kitchen Witch **21**
Le Garage **17**
Louisiana Music Factory **18**
Lucullus **10**
Meyer the Hatter **2**
Muse **13**
The Outlet Collection at Riverwalk Marketplace **5**
Queork **14**
Rubenstein's **3**
Southern Candymakers **8, 15**

Shopping A to Z

Antiques

★★ Keil's Antiques ROYAL STREET Established in 1899 and run by the founder's great-grandson, Keil's has a considerable collection of 18th-and 19th-century French and English furniture, chandeliers, and jewelry. *325 Royal St.* ☎ *504/522-4552. www.keilsantiques.com. Map p 75.*

★ Lucullus FRENCH QUARTER A wonderful collection of culinary antiques and furnishings to "complement the grand pursuits of cooking, dining, and imbibing." All manner of china, silverware, oyster plates, and absinthe accoutrements.

610 Chartres St. ☎ *504/528-9620. www.lucullusantiques.com. Map p 74.*

★ Magazine Antique Mall MAGAZINE STREET Booth after booth of independent dealers with everything from 18th- and 19th-century furnishings to music boxes, artworks, collectibles, and antique toys. Plenty of affordable used clothes and mid-century goods. *3017 Magazine St.* ☎ *504/896-9994. Map p 73.*

★★★ M.S. Rau Antiques ROYAL STREET For sheer jaw-dropping outrageousness, walk through this opulent collection and ogle away. We're fond of the walking sticks, cave bear skeleton, lavish

French Quarter Shopping

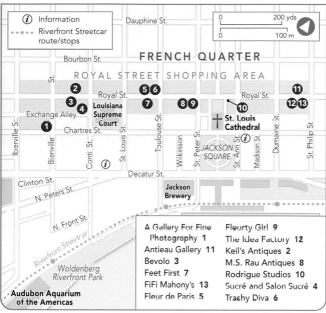

A Gallery For Fine Photography **1**
Antieau Gallery **11**
Bevolo **3**
Feet First **7**
FiFi Mahony's **13**
Fleur de Paris **5**
Fleurty Girl **9**
The Idea Factory **12**
Keil's Antiques **2**
M.S. Rau Antiques **8**
Rodrigue Studios **10**
Sucré and Salon Sucré **4**
Trashy Diva **6**

silver service in many-drawered cabinets, insanely ornate furnishings, and monstrous gems. *630 Royal St.* ☎ *504/523-5660. www. rauantiques.com. Map p 75.*

Beauty Products & Cosmetics
★★★ Aidan Gill for Men
MAGAZINE STREET/CENTRAL BUSINESS DISTRICT Long before the facial hair frenzy and male grooming renaissance, Aidan Gill championed the art of gentlemanliness. Sharp-dressed men and those in need of gifts for same will find luxurious implements and accessories. Superb salon services too. *2026 Magazine St.* ☎ *504/587-9090. 550 Fulton St.* ☎ *504/566-4903. www.aidangillformen.com. Map p 73.*

★★ Hové Parfumeur CHARTRES
STREET For more than 75 years the family-run Hové has created original perfumes, colognes, body oils, lotions, and soaps from original and classic Southern fragrances such as Tea Olive and Vetivert. Great, easy-to-pack gifts. *434 Chartres St.* ☎ *504/525-7827. www. hoveparfumeur.com. Map p 74.*

Books & Stationery
★★ Beckham's Bookshop
FRENCH QUARTER With 60,000 volumes carefully collected by the store's owners jamming two floors, beloved Beckham's has been a pillar of the Quarter's thriving indie bookshop scene since 1967. *228 Decatur St.* ☎ *504/522-9875. www. beckhamsbookshop.com. Map p 74.*

★★ Crescent City Books

CENTRAL BUSINESS DISTRICT A gorgeous, eminently browsable antiquarian collection for the seriously literate, with an emphasis on history, philosophy, and local interest. *124 Baronne St.* ☎ *504/524-4997. www.crescentcitybooks.com. Map p 74.*

★★★ Faulkner House Books

FRENCH QUARTER That Nobel Prize–winner William Faulkner lived here while writing his early works is but one literary morsel in this perfect, one-room bookshop. Gracious advice and a judicious selection of titles by Southern authors, best sellers, and stunning first editions make manifest the art of bookselling. *624 Pirate's Alley.* ☎ *504/524-2940. www. faulknerhousebooks.com. Map p 74.*

★★ Kitchen Witch MID-CITY

In a town of foodies, cooks, and eaters of all interests and proficiencies, this quirky cookbook store with nearly 10,000 volumes, from the ultra-rare to the just-released, is the rainbow's end. *1452 N. Broad St.* ☎ *504/528-8382. www.kwcookbooks.com. Map p 74.*

Clothing & Shoes
★★ Dirty Coast MAGAZINE

STREET/FRENCH QUARTER For souvenir tees, skip the raunchy offerings on Bourbon Street in favor of these utterly witty, eye-catching, and original T-shirt designs (painted in the city), like the "Crawfish Pi," with the Greek symbol composed of a tasty pile of mudbugs, and "504Ever." *5631 Magazine St.* ☎ *504/324-3745. 2121 Chartres St.* ☎ *504/324-6459. www. dirtycoast.com. Map p 74.*

★★ Dollz and Dames DECATUR

STREET If the Frenchmen Street jitterbugging scene has released your inner pin-up gal, this is your store. The vintage-y frocks and custom T-strap dance-style shoes

Hové Parfumeur has a scent for just about everyone.

make for darling date wear, but we'd wear them any time. *216 Decatur St.* ☎ *504/522-5472. www.dollzanddames.com. Map p 74.*

★★ Feet First ROYAL STREET/

MAGAZINE STREET Shoes, handbags, and accessories galore, with new inventory added every week. The crowded shelves feature designers (including Michael Kors and Kate Spade) plus local favorites NOLA Couture and Citizen NOLA. *4122 Magazine St.* ☎ *504/899-6800. 526 Royal St.* ☎ *504/569-0005. www.feetfirststores.com. Map p 73.*

★★ Fifi Mahony's ROYAL

STREET Wig wackiness? Sure! Cutesy or crazy, have the hair you've always wanted, for a day, a party, or a lifetime. Outrageous custom pieces and full salon services available. *934 Royal St.* ☎ *504/525-4343. www.fifimahonys.com. Map p 75.*

★★★ Fleur de Paris ROYAL

STREET We seriously covet the 1920s and 1930s elegance here, from hand-blocked, stylishly trimmed hats to luscious stockings and couture gowns. Works of art, they are. *523 Royal St.* ☎ *504/525-1899. www.fdphats.com. Map p 75.*

★★★ Fleurty Girl FRENCH

QUARTER/MAGAZINE STREET

A fave shop for the superbly clever, NOLA-centric T-shirts ("Keep Calm and Carry a Go-cup") and gifts. The $5 tea towels and water meter coasters are great stocking stuffer souvenirs. *632 St. Peter St. ☎ 504/304-5529. 3117 Magazine St. ☎ 504/301-2557. www.fleurtygirl.net. Map p 75.*

★★ **Le Garage** DECATUR STREET An ever-changing selection of retro and vintage clothing and oddball antiques pack the small space. Ideal for last-minute costume needs. *1234 Decatur St. ☎ 504/522-6639. Map p 74.*

★★ **Lili Vintage** UPTOWN Everything in this dollhouse—from crinolines to cardigans and Victoriana to Audreyana—is pristinely selected, beautifully merchandised, in good condition, and fairly priced. Hit it when that just-right beaded purse or Pucci print is in for that tingly shopping rush. *3329 Magazine St. ☎ 504/931-6848. www.lilivintage. com. Map p 73.*

★★★ **Meyer the Hatter** CENTRAL BUSINESS DISTRICT Family-owned for more than 100 years, this haberdashery's huge selection of fine hats and caps goes well beyond trendy fedoras. Let them

Couture clothes at Fleur de Paris.

fuss over you and pick out the proper chapeau—these hat whisperers know just how to top every head. *120 St. Charles Ave. ☎ 504/525-1048. www. meyerthehatter.com. Map p 74.*

★★ **Muse** FRENCH QUARTER Gentlemen, should the city and the spirit move you to seek a metallic paisley, madras plaid, or seersucker sport jacket, here's your grail. Ladies, the fine frock selection here will have him (and you) strutting even prouder. *532 St. Peter St. ☎ 504/522-8738. www.muse inspiredfashion.com. Map p 74.*

★★ **Rubenstein's** CENTRAL BUSINESS DISTRICT For 90 years, this hallowed haberdasher has outfitted proper New Orleans gents in custom suits, fine menswear, and perfect prepwear. Their pros will dress you to the nines and fit you to a T. Quick-turnaround tailoring gets you Galatoire's-ready. *102 St. Charles Ave. ☎ 504/581-6666. www.ruben steinsneworleans.com. Map p 74.*

★★★ **Trashy Diva** MAGAZINE STREET/ROYAL STREET The utterly untrashy 1940s and '50s inspired clothes and shoes are flirty, curve-flattering, and appealing to both Bettys and Goths. Similar-era shoes, va-va-voom corsets and lingerie, and good sales, too. *537 Royal St. ☎ 504/522-4233. 2048 Magazine St. ☎ 504/299-8777. www. trashydiva.com. Map p 73 and p 75.*

Food, Chocolates & Wine
★★ **Keife & Co.** CENTRAL BUSINESS DISTRICT If you just can't leave the room, Keife will deliver a basket with gourmet meats, cheeses, and wine to your Central Business District hotel room. If you *can* get out, grab a bottle on your way to the restaurant. Great selection; even better service. *801 Howard Ave. ☎ 504/523-7272. www. keifeandco.com. Map p 73.*

The Best Shopping

Finding the perfect hat at Meyer the Hatter.

★ **Martin Wine Cellar** UPTOWN The massive array of wine, spirits, champagne, craft beer, and gourmet items impresses; the terrific full-service deli appeases. *3827 Baronne St. ☎ 504/899-7411. www. martinwine.com. Map p 73.*

★★ **Southern Candymakers** DECATUR STREET Our top choice for pralines; they're just extra creamylicious and come in many flavors. A box of the toothsome pecan caramel tortues (turtles) or some gator-shaped chocolates help sate the family's or office mates' travel envy. *334 Decatur St. ☎ 504/523-5544. 1010 Decatur St. ☎ 504/525-6170. www.southerncandymakers. com. Map p 74.*

★★★ **Sucre and Salon Sucre** MAGAZINE STREET and FRENCH QUARTER The high-end confections, sherbet-hued macarons, and gorgeous chocolates are ideal for gifts or an afternoon indulgence at these stylish cafes. We're partial to the minicakes and Modbar coffee at the FQ Salon. *3025 Magazine St. ☎ 504/520-8311. 622 Conti St. ☎ 504/267-7098. www.shopsucre. com. Map p 73 and p 75.*

Galleries
★★★ **A Gallery for Fine Photography** FRENCH QUARTER Even if you can't afford a signed Ansel Adams, Sebastião Salgado, or Herman Leonard print, it's worth stepping inside to view the world-class collection, which includes

Southern artists and subjects as well as a fine book selection. *241 Chartres St. ☎ 504/568-1313. www. agallery.com. Map p 75.*

★★★ **Antieau Gallery** ROYAL STREET/MAGAZINE STREET We adore the supremely clever Chris Roberts-Antieau's whimsical sewn works that riff on current events and social mores—and her darker, macabre snow globes. A second gallery is at 4532 Magazine St. *927 Royal St. ☎ 504/304-0849. www. antieaugallery.com. Map p 75.*

★★ **Arthur Roger Gallery** WAREHOUSE Roger pioneered the city's Warehouse District and fine-art scene here some 30+ years ago, tying the local community to the New York art world. He's still blazing trails with always-progressive shows featuring regional and far-flung artists. *432 Julia St. ☎ 504/522-1999. www.arthur rogergallery.com. Map p 73.*

★★★ **Christopher Porche-West** BYWATER These stunning portrait photographs are themselves works of art, but when sculpted and framed within magnificent assemblages of architectural remnants, mechanical parts, natural materials, and found oddities, they are singular statement pieces. *3201 Burgundy St. ☎ 504/947-3880. www.porche-west.com. Map p 74.*

Dr. Bob Studios BYWATER The iconic, bottlecap-edged "Be Nice or Leave" folk art signs are here in every size, shape, and color—and if he's around, Dr. Bob (Shaffer)

Macarons at Sucre.

Private torch-working lessons at New Orleans Glassworks and Printmaking Studio.

himself offers plenty of additional color. *3027 Chartres St.* ☎ *504/945-2225. www.drbobart.net. Map p 74.*

★★ **New Orleans Glassworks and Printmaking Studio** MAGAZINE STREET Hippie and hipster artisans make and sell blown and sculpted glassworks, Venetian paper, and other works. Cool demonstrations and hands-on classes for visitors make for a unique vacation experience. *727 Magazine St.* ☎ *504/529-7279. www.neworleans glassworks.com. Map p 73.*

★ **Rodrigue Studios** ROYAL STREET George Rodrigue toiled away painting moody and critically acclaimed Cajun landscapes, until finding fame and fortune when he started painting his beloved pup in bright blue. The critically panned but publicly embraced Blue Dog is here in umpteen sizes and scenarios. *730 Royal St.* ☎ *504/581-4244. www. georgerodrigue.com. Map p 75.*

Housewares, Furnishings & Art
★★★ **Bevolo** ROYAL STREET Stop in to see these gorgeous copper gaslight lanterns, a local tradition, being hand-fabricated by master craftsmen. Who knows—you might decide to amp up your home's curb appeal (or opt for a miniature votive version). *318 Royal St.* ☎ *504/522-9485. www. bevolo.com. Map p 75.*

★ **Hazelnut** MAGAZINE STREET Well-selected home furnishings capped by a collection in a custom, New Orleans–themed toile pattern are on tap at Bryan Batt's shop (he of *Mad Men* fame—and a native New Orleanean). *5515 Magazine St.* ☎ *504/891-2424. www.hazelnut neworleans.com. Map p 73.*

★ **Queork** FRENCH QUARTER All-cork merchandise seems a strange concept, until you spy that want-want-want iPhone case. Then it's a slippery slope to a cork belt and cork-upholstered furniture. It's surprisingly durable, they say, and undoubtedly unique. *838 Chartres St.* ☎ *504/481-4910. www.queork. com. Map p 74.*

Jewelry
★ **Jose Balli** FRENCH QUARTER STREET Balli's rough-hewn designs reflecting his Cajun culture are carved and transferred via wax mold onto silver charms, bracelets, earrings, and more, and paired with refined semi-precious gems and pearls—with quite lovely results.*621 Chartres St.* ☎ *504/522-1770. www. joseballi.com. Map p 74.*

★★ **Marion Cage** MAGAZINE STREET Cage's ultrafine, exquisitely wrought work in clean lines of matte rose and yellow gold, rhodium, leather, and hardwoods is popular with collectors in Paris, New York, and her native New Orleans. *3007 Magazine St.* ☎ *504/891-8848 www.marioncage.com. Map p 73.*

★★ **Mignon Faget** MAGAZINE STREET Local artist and treasure Faget creates fine gold, silver, and bronze jewelry incorporating fleur de lis, other Louisiana icons, and shapes plucked from nature and technology. Various houseware objects too—all superb gifts for self or other. *3801 Magazine St.* ☎ *504/891-2005. 333 Canal St.* ☎ *504/524-2973. www. mignonfaget.com. Map p 73.*

George Rodrigue is most famous for his "Blue Dog" paintings.

Music

★★★ Domino Sound MID-CITY

This funky, tucked-away vinyl Heaven (with some cassettes) is for you if you're into reggaeton, Northern soul, world music oddities, and all things Sun Ra. And that's just a start. *2557 Bayou Road.* ☎ *504/309-0871. www.dominosoundrecords.com. Cash only. Map p 74.*

★★ Euclid Records BYWATER

This younger-than-it-feels waxworks shop (sistah of the iconic St. Louis store) stocks vintage platters from every era and gobs of local goods. *3301 Chartres St.* ☎ *504/947-4348. www.euclidnola.com. Map p 74.*

★★★ Louisiana Music Factory

FRENCH QUARTER   *The* place to get yourself informed about and stocked with New Orleans music, with helpful staff and a large selection of regional music—including Cajun, zydeco, R&B, jazz, blues, and gospel—plus books, posters, and T-shirts and live performances on Saturdays. *421 Frenchmen St.* ☎ *504/586-1094. www.louisiana musicfactory.com. Map p 74.*

Shopping Centers

★ Canal Place FRENCH QUARTER

Upscale chains including Saks Fifth Avenue, Tiffany, Armani, and Anthropologie populate this sparkling, well-air-conditioned mall at the foot of Canal Street. The top floor has movie theaters. *333 Canal St.* ☎ *504/522-9200. www.theshops atcanalplace.com. Map p 74.*

★ French Market FRENCH

QUARTER   These historic, open-air shops offer foodstuffs, clothes, and all manner of New Orleans memorabilia to savor or ship. The flea market section has cheap trinkets and a smattering of actual artworks. A stage for live music or cooking demos and food and beverage booths entertain. *1235 N. Peters St.* ☎ *504/596-3420. www.french market.org. Map p 74.*

★★ Frenchmen Art Market

MARIGNY   Good selection of artworks, jewelry, and clothes, mostly handcrafted in some form and reasonably priced. A great addition to (and diversion from) the Frenchmen Street madness. *619 Frenchmen St.* ☎ *504/941-1149. www.frenchmen artmarket.com. Map p 74.*

★ Outlet Collection at River-walk Marketplace CENTRAL

BUSINESS DISTRICT   Neiman Marcus Last Call, Steve Madden, Kenneth Cole, and 75 other outlet stores fill the three-story mall. Bargains are a bonus when you can walk from the French Quarter, shop with a daiquiri in hand, and enjoy a sublime view of the Mississippi from a mall food court. *500 Port of New Orleans Place.* ☎ *504/522-1555. www.riverwalkmarketplace.com. Map p 74.*

Toys

★★ The Idea Factory ROYAL

STREET   Wonderfully throwback wooden toys of real substance, like alphabet and number blocks, trains, and pull toys. *924 Royal St.* ☎ *504/524-5195. www.ideafactory neworleans.com. Map p 75.* ●

5

The Best of the
Outdoors

City Park

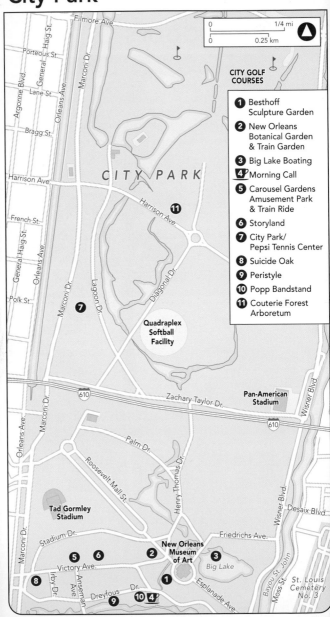

CITY GOLF COURSES

1 Besthoff Sculpture Garden

2 New Orleans Botanical Garden & Train Garden

3 Big Lake Boating

4 Morning Call

5 Carousel Gardens Amusement Park & Train Ride

6 Storyland

7 City Park/ Pepsi Tennis Center

8 Suicide Oak

9 Peristyle

10 Popp Bandstand

11 Couterie Forest Arboretum

CITY PARK

Quadraplex Softball Facility

Pan-American Stadium

Tad Gormley Stadium

New Orleans Museum of Art

Big Lake

St. Louis Cemetery No. 3

Previous page: Audubon Park.

In glorious **City Park (1,300 acres),** check out the enormous oak tree between the sculpture garden and Morning Call cafe. Once the sight of duels-to-the-death, it's now popular with betrothing lovebirds. And that about sums up this immense, beautifully landscaped space—it's got everything. Besides vast lawns and paths for exercising, thinking, or just gazing at the graceful swans and moss-dripping live oaks (the largest collection in the world!), it's a treasure trove of culture and activity, with botanical gardens; lagoons and ponds for turtle-watching or boating; bike paths and rentals; a terrific tennis center; two New Orleans–themed miniature golf courses; a bandstand with summertime concerts; sports stadiums; a miniature train city and a not-so-miniature one you can ride in; a kids-sized amusement park, complete with old-school carousel; and the treasured **New Orleans Museum of Art** (p 14). Some of the handsome bridges and other structures were designed under the architecturally fruitful 1930s-era Works Progress Administration (WPA) program, and many worthy special events are held here throughout the year (including Christmastime, when the mighty oaks are strung with light displays—a magical sight). It's truly fabulous. START: **1 Palm Dr., bounded by City Park Avenue and Canal, Robert E. Lee, and Wisner Boulevards. Take the Canal Streetcar "City Park/Museum" line. The last stop lets you off at N. Carrollton and Esplanade avenues, the entrance to City Park.**

❶ ★★★ kids Besthoff Sculpture Garden. Five serene, landscaped acres (2 hectares) contrast with the clean lines of 60 contemporary sculptures, including works by George Segal, Henry Moore, and a version of Robert Indiana's famous *LOVE* pop art. Besthoffs commissioned Jean-Michel

Figures in the Besthoff Sculpture Garden.

Othoniel's whimsical *Tree of Necklaces,* giant glass bead necklaces suspended from live-oak branches, evoking the beads hanging from trees along the Mardi Gras parade routes. Kids can ramble (but not clamber) while grown-ups regard. ⏱ *1 hr. 1 Dueling Oaks Dr., adjacent to the New Orleans Museum of Art.* ☎ *504/658-4100. www.noma.org. Free admission. Mon–Fri 10am–6pm, Sat–Sun 10am–5pm.*

❷ ★★ New Orleans Botanical Garden and Train Garden. A stunning collection of orchids, staghorn ferns, bromeliads, and many more (including our favorite—the 4-foot [1.2m] diameter, flowering water lilies) are carefully and exquisitely cultivated in one of the few remaining public gardens designed by the WPA in the 1930s. The dramatic, glass-domed Conservatory of Two Sisters is at the center of the Art Deco–era gardens, fountains, ponds, and sculptures. Tucked away here is the Historic Train Garden, an extraordinary, unique model of New Orleans's neighborhoods, complete with tiny replica streetcars and trains made entirely out of botanical materials. ⏱ *1 hr. 5 Victory Ave.* ☎ *504/483-9386. www.neworleanscitypark.com/botanical-garden. Admission $6 adults, $3 children 5–12; free for kids 4 and under. Daily 10am–5pm.*

❸ ★★ Big Lake Boating.
Paddle out in relaxing or more energetic fashion via canoe, pedal boat, or paddleboard and explore the lake and lagoons. You might see swans, ducks, geese, turtles, frogs, and fish—thankfully, no gators. ⏱ *1 hr. City Park Big Lake at Esplanade Ave. Boathouse is lakeside near Friedrichs Ave.* ☎ *504/224-2601. Rentals $19–$30. Nov–Feb Sat–Sun 11am–5pm.; Mar–Oct Sat–Sun 11am–6pm.*

❹ ★★ Morning Call
Did we mention you can get beignets in City Park any time of the day or night? Jambalaya, gumbo, and other specialties too. This new location of the historic cafe is open 24 hours. *Timken Center (old Casino Building), 57 Dreyfous Dr.* ☎ *504/300-1157. Cash only. $.*

❺ ★★ kids Carousel Gardens Amusement Park and Train Ride.
Just right for younger kids, who will love the bumper cars, a Red Baron miniplane, a Tilt-A-Whirl, a 40-foot (12m) fun slide, a Ferris wheel, and more. Kids of all ages and sizes also love the "flying horses" on the antique wooden carousel. Built in 1910, it is on the National Register of Historic Places and just one of only 100 left in the country. A miniature train takes

riders on a 2½-mile (4km) trip through the park. ⏱ *45 min. Dreyfous Dr.* ☎ *504/483-9432. www.neworleanscitypark.com. Admission $4 ages 3 and up, free for 2 and under; rides $4 each, unlimited-ride band $18. Mid-Mar–Mid-Nov Fri–Sun 11am–6pm; extended hours June–Aug.*

❻ kids ★ Storyland.
More than 25 storybook-themed play areas feature colorful characters hand-sculpted by Mardi Gras float artists. Kids can climb in and out of Captain Hook's pirate ship, do a jig with the Three Little Pigs, explore the mouth of a whale with Pinocchio, or race up Jack & Jill's Hill. ⏱ *1 hr. Dreyfous Dr., next to Carousel Gardens.* ☎ *504/483-5402. Admission $4, free for 2 and under. Daily 10am–5pm.*

❼ City Park/Pepsi Tennis Center.
New in 2015 and one of the largest public tennis facilities in the South, featuring 26 lighted clay and hard courts. *5900 Marconi Dr.* ☎ *504/483-9383. www.neworleanscitypark.com. $12–$15 per hr. Mon–Thurs 7am–10pm, Fri–Sun 7am–7pm.*

Kids make friends with a Storyland dragon.

Kayaking Bayou St. John

The unique perspective of a kayak along Bayou St. John is a more unusual and active way to learn city lore, as well as a sublime way to explore some historic neighborhoods. Tours run by Kaya-kitiyat (☎ 985/778-5034; www.kayakitiyat.com) range from an easy 2-hour amble to a more intense, 4-hour workout. Tours cost $40 and up and meet at Esplanade Avenue and Moss Street, just across Bayou St. John from City Park. No bathroom stops, so plan ahead.

⑧ Suicide Oak. Measuring more than 22 feet (6.6m) in circumference and 65 feet (20m) high with a 124-foot (37m) crown, Suicide Oak is one of the oldest and largest live oaks in the park. In the late 1800s and early 1900s, many despondent people chose to end their lives here. After the Huey P. Long Bridge was built in 1935, it replaced Sui-cide Oak's sordid purpose. Though City Park lost 2,000 trees to the post-Katrina flooding, this one sur-vived. The enormous limb lying beneath the tree, estimated to be more than 150 years old, fell in the 1980s. ⏱ 10 min. Corner of Marconi Dr. and Victory Ave.

⑨ Peristyle. Built in 1907, this elegant neoclassical structure with massive Ionic columns originally served as a dance pavilion. Four concrete lions guard the structure, whose steps lead down to the bayou, where graceful swans and geese and ducks will shamelessly

barter a photo for food. The Peri-style continues to set the scene for countless weddings, cocktail par-ties, picnics, and moonlit dances, of course. ⏱ 15 min. Dreyfous Dr. overlooking Bayou Metairie.

⑩ Popp Bandstand. Erected in 1917, the bandstand remains popu-lar for outdoor concerts. U.S. Marine bandleader John Philip Sousa performed here in 1928. The huge live oak to the left of the Peri-style is now known as the Sousa Oak. ⏱ 10 min. Dreyfous Dr. over-looking Bayou Metairie.

⑪ Couterie Forest Arbore-tum. More than 280 bird species, from egrets to water thrushes, make for a birder's paradise. The 30-acre (12-hectare) park features birding, hiking, and fishing (permits and your own gear are required). ⏱ ½–1 hr. Harrison Ave. at Diagonal Dr. turnaround. ☎ 504/482-4888. www.neworleanscitypark.com. Free admission. Open daily 8am–6pm.

Mississippi River

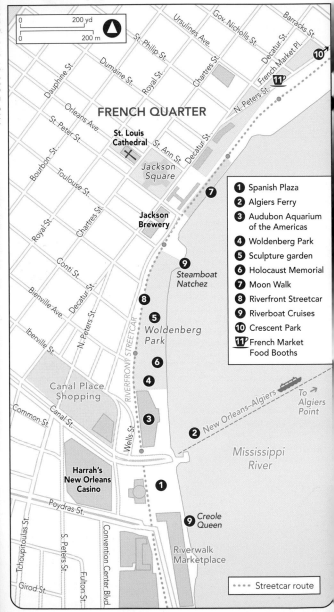

1. Spanish Plaza
2. Algiers Ferry
3. Audubon Aquarium of the Americas
4. Woldenberg Park
5. Sculpture garden
6. Holocaust Memorial
7. Moon Walk
8. Riverfront Streetcar
9. Riverboat Cruises
10. Crescent Park
11. French Market Food Booths

FRENCH QUARTER

St. Louis Cathedral

Jackson Square

Jackson Brewery

Steamboat Natchez

Woldenberg Park

Canal Place Shopping

Harrah's New Orleans Casino

Creole Queen

Riverwalk Marketplace

Mississippi River

New Orleans–Algiers

To Algiers Point

RIVERFRONT STREETCAR

····· Streetcar route

It's why we're here. Early settlers recognized that the swampy high ground tucked into a "crescent" of the Mississippi River would make for a perfect international port, so the original Crescent City—the French Quarter—was built alongside the Mighty Muddy in 1718. Today it's a major port city, and the riverfront remains a bustling public thoroughfare. Catch the sweeping views of the mythical waterway from land or ferry, with lush landscaping and evocative sculptures along the walking path as birds and street musicians fill the humid air with song. START: Spanish Plaza, 1 Poydras St.

1 **Spanish Plaza.** Perhaps one of the most underrated romantic spots in the city, this beautifully tiled fountain with a view of the Mississippi was given to the city during the U.S. bicentennial in 1976 as a gift from Spain. Occasionally you'll see a couple get married here, then disappear back into the French Quarter. (Shoppers, of course, know to disappear into the outlet mall next door for some serious shopping; see p 80.) ⏱ *20 min. 1 Poydras St. at Mississippi River, beside Outlet Collection at Riverwalk Marketplace. Free admission. Daily 10am–6pm.*

Views of the Mississippi and St. Louis Cathedral from the Algiers ferry.

2 ★ **Algiers Ferry.** It's not historic or architecturally pleasing, but a quick jaunt across the river to Algiers Point on this pedestrian ferry takes you to a historic neighborhood and provides stellar, budget-rate views of the city skyline. ⏱ *5 min. Foot of Canal St.* ☎ *504/376-8180 or 504/250-9110. www.nolaferries.com. $2 each way. Mon–Thurs 6:15am–9:15pm, Fri*

6:15am–11:15pm, Sat 10:45am–11:15pm, Sun 10:45am–9:15pm; leaves every 30 min.

3 ★★ kids **Aquarium of the Americas.** Whoever said "Learning is fun!" was right. The focus here is on the Mississippi and Gulf of Mexico waterways and wildlife,

Audubon Aquarium of the Americas.

but we also love the huge interior rain forest, complete with birds and piranhas, and being able to peer below the surface of a swamp. There's plenty of interactivity, a fine frog exhibit, a rare albino gator, a manta-ray touch tank, and an irresistible outdoor splash fountain. See p 45. ◷ *1–3 hr. 1 Canal St.* ☎ *504/565-3033. www.audubon natureinstitute.org/aquarium. Admission $25 adults, $19 seniors and children 2–12. Daily 10am–5pm.*

④ ★ Woldenberg Park. This 20-acre (8-hectare) park running alongside the river is named after local philanthropist and civic leader Malcolm Woldenberg. ◷ *30 min. Along river btw. aquarium and Jackson Square. Free admission.*

⑤ ★ Sculpture garden. This informal sculpture garden almost melds into the scenery, but it's worth one's attention for some important artistic works. Favorites include Robert Schoen's Carrera-marble figure *Old Man River,* a fitting tribute to the breadth and depth of the Mississippi. ◷ *30 min. In Woldenberg Park. Free admission.*

⑥ Holocaust Memorial. Dedicated in 2003, this affecting, colorful memorial was rendered by Israeli sculptor Yaacov Agam. Walk around slowly and pay attention to the way the art changes as your

viewing angle does. ◷ *15 min. In Woldenberg Park. Free admission.*

⑦ kids ★★ Moon Walk. The platform up the stairs next to Café du Monde offers picture-perfect views of the Mississippi River, the Crescent City Connection, and Jackson Square. No selfie sticks, please. See p 46. ◷ *20 min. Across from Jackson Square along Mississippi River.*

⑧ Riverfront streetcar. Cherry-red vintage-looking streetcars run nearly 2 miles (3.2km) along the river, past old wharves and warehouses behind the French Market, giving you a glimpse of the glory days of river-run industry. ◷ *20 min. Thalia St. to Esplanade Ave.* ☎ *504/248-3900. www.norta.com. Fare $1.25 one-way. See p 165.*

⑨ kids ★★ Riverboat rides. Okay all you Huck Finn (or Tyrone Power) wannabees, here's your chance to ply the deep waters of Old Miss. The steamboat *Natchez,* a marvelous three-deck sternwheeler, re-creates the 19th-century version that held the record for fastest steamship until the *Robert E. Lee* famously whipped it in 1870. Now it takes leisurely jazz cruises with a bit of history thrown in and optional meals. On the smaller *Creole Queen,* Don Vappie, our favorite local banjo player, leads the band

The Creole Queen.

Touring the Swamps

Away from the Mississippi, a tour of spookily beautiful swamps can be a hoot and a holler when the gators come right alongside the boats — no fools, they know where the snacks are! As long as it's not during hibernation season, you're gonna see 'em, along with elegant waterfowl, turtles, and perhaps even a feral hog or freaky nutria rat. But it's a pleasant float any time of year, and learning about how this unique ecosystem contributes to the local culture and economy is quite interesting. Most boats are covered but call to confirm, especially if rain or extreme sun is forecast.

We like the expert local captains and Southern hospitality with **Pearl River Eco Tours ★★★,** located northeast of New Orleans (☎ 985/649-4200; www.pearlriverecotours.com). Their night tours are supremely cool, even if they do slightly freak us out. The 2-hour offering is $25 for adults, $15 for children under 12 (with transportation to the swamp, it's $52/$32.50).

For something with a little more action, try the speed demons at **Airboat Adventures ★★★,** south of the city (☎ 888/467-9267; www.airboatadventures.com). Tours are $55 and up ($75 with transportation). For both outfits, call ahead for times and reservations.

during the 7:30pm jazz cruise; a daytime Historical River Cruise, stops downriver at Chalmette Battlefield, site of the Battle of New Orleans. Both ships have outside decks, comfortable inside lounges, and great, big, water-churning paddlewheels out back. Drinks and so-so food are optional. ⓧ *2-3 hr. Steamboat Natchez: Docked at the end of Toulouse St. behind Jax Brewery. ☎ 504/586-8777. www.steamboatnatchez.com. Tickets $31–$48 adults, $12.25–$23.50 children 6–12. Creole Queen: Docked near the aquarium and the end of Canal St. ☎ 504/529-4567. www.creolequeen.com. Tickets $28–$44 adults, $13–$20 children 6–12. Food and drinks additional on both boats. Call for schedules.*

🔟 ★ **Crescent Park.** Cross the wheelchair-accessible bridge at Elysian Fields Avenue, or the arc-shaped "rusty rainbow" bridge in the Bywater, to stroll or bike this recently opened linear park and events space. The pristine, 1.5-mile (2.4km) riverfront park is a photographer's delight with stunning views and lush native foliage. ⓧ *30 min. or more. Access via bridges at N. Peters St. just east of Elysian Fields Ave., or at Piety and Chartres sts. Free. 8am–6pm; later during some special events.*

🔢 ★★ **French Market Food Booths.** Among the much-improved offerings here lately, we're loving the fare from Continental Provisions and Meals from the Heart. Other stalls have fresh oysters and decent cocktails. Choose wisely and often, we say. *1100 N. Peters St. Continental Provisions: www.facebook.com/continentalprov, ☎ 504/407-3437; Meals from the Heart: www.mealsfromtheheartcafe.com, ☎ 504/525-1953. $.*

Audubon Park

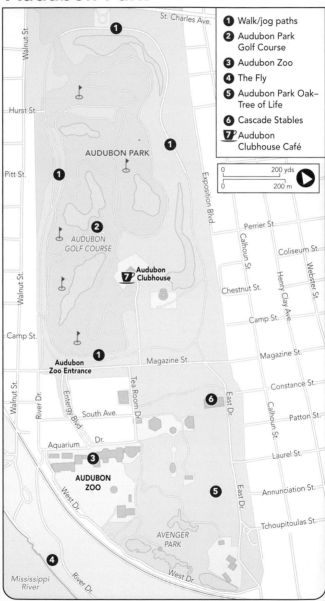

1 Walk/jog paths
2 Audubon Park Golf Course
3 Audubon Zoo
4 The Fly
5 Audubon Park Oak–Tree of Life
6 Cascade Stables
7 Audubon Clubhouse Café

As a college student and Uptown resident, I often sought quiet refuge in Audubon Park. This peaceful, 340-acre urban respite across from Loyola and Tulane universities is set between St. Charles Avenue and the Mississippi River on land once owned by city founder Jean-Baptiste Le Moyne. Later a sugar plantation and the site of the 1884 World's Fair, the park is named after famed naturalist and artist John James Audubon. His mother was a French/Spanish Creole from Louisiana, and he created much of his art in the Pelican State. Today, students, locals, and visitors come here to enjoy the wide-open spaces, oak-shaded lawns, and perfect picnic spots. Tennis, golf, swimming, and the acclaimed Audubon Zoo attract the young and the not-so-young. START: **6500 St. Charles Ave. Take the St. Charles streetcar to the Tulane/Loyola stop.**

Seal show at the Audubon Zoo.

❶ Walk/Jog paths Follow the nearly 2-mile (3.2km) asphalt track and 18 exercise stations shaded by centuries-old live oak trees

dripping with Spanish moss, and enjoy colorful year-round landscaping and dreamy lagoons filled with birds, turtles, and fish. ⏱ *1 hr. Open daily sunrise–sunset.*

❷ Audubon Park Golf Course. *Golf Digest* named this challenging, awfully pretty par 62 executive course the best golf course over 100 years old in the country. ⏱ *2–4 hr. 6500 Magazine St. (btw. Walnut & Calhoun sts.).* ☎ *504/861-2537. www.auduboninstitute.org/golf. Open Mon 10am–6:30pm; Tues–Fri 7am–6:30pm; Sat–Sun 6:30am–6:30pm. Green fees $20–$65.*

❸ ★★ kids Audubon Zoo. This right-sized, delightful zoo is small enough to be manageable, but with some 1,800 animals (including

Walkers enjoy a quiet stroll in Audubon Park.

Biking and Strolling the City

This flat, relatively compact town is ideal for two-wheeling (potholes aside) and leisurely walks. We like the sturdy American-made cruisers from **Freewheelin' Bike Tours ★★★,** a half-dozen blocks west of Jackson Square (325 Burgundy St.; ☎ 504/522-4368; www.neworleansbiketour.com), whose well-informed guides show off the sights, sounds, and cemeteries. (You might even see where one of the guides' great-grandparents are buried.) They offer French Quarter and Uptown tours with all the highlights—including a stop for a snoball on hot days. Tours run $49, including bike and helmet. Call for times and reservations.

Lafitte Greenway, an ambitious post-Katrina success story, is a new linear park with pedestrian and bike paths, sporting fields, and play spaces. Built over an abandoned railway, it runs from the edge of the French Quarter through the Faubourg Tremé and up to Mid-City. The trailhead is at Basin and St. Louis streets.

rare and endangered species and a new elephant enclosure), it's big enough to cover all the important zoo bases. Cool Zoo, a splash park with an inner-tube river, is a perfect hot-day diversion (bring swimwear!). ⏱ 2–3 hr. 6500 Magazine St. ☎ 504/861-2537. www.audubon institute.org/zoo. Admission $20 adults, $15 seniors and children 2–12; add $5 for Cool Zoo access. Daily 10am–5pm (till 6pm Sat–Sun).

④ ★ The Fly. This small but scenic riverside park is popular with locals for picnics, ball games,

Carousel at the Audubon Zoo.

rendezvous points, and watching boat and barge traffic along the Mississippi. It's officially "The Riverview," but locals call it "The Fly." *River Drive off Magazine St., along the Mississippi River.*

⑤ kids Audubon Park Oak. Measuring more than 35 feet (11m) around and 165 feet (50m) across its crown, it's an impressive oak that's deserving of your respect (and a selfie). ⏱ 15 min. Btw. The Fly and Magazine St.

⑥ kids Cascade Stables. See Audubon Park from the saddle on a gentle, guided horseback ride around its perimeter. One of the few steed rental places around. ⏱ 1 hr. 700 East Dr. ☎ 504/891-2246. www. cascadestables.net. $40 per trail ride. Age 8 and up; reservations preferred. Fri Noon–4pm; Sat–Sun 10am–4pm.

⑦ Audubon Clubhouse Café. *Convenient and pretty brunchy/lunchy spot set amid the park's gorgeous greenery.* ☎ 504/212-5285. $$. ●

Dining Best Bets

Best **Celebrity-Chef Meal**
★★★ Emeril's $$$ *800 Tchoupitoulas St. (p 102)*

Best **Classic Creole Restaurant**
★★ Arnaud's $$$ *813 Bienville St. (p 99)*

Best **Modern Creole**
★★★ Coquette $$ *2800 Magazine St. (p 100)*

Best **Diner**
★★ Camellia Grill $ *626 S. Carrollton Ave. (p 100)*

Best **Burger**
★ Port of Call $ *838 Esplanade Ave. (p 106)*

Best **Fried Chicken**
★★ Willie Mae's Scotch House $ *2401 St. Ann St. & 7457 St. Charles Ave. (p 108)*

Best **Bakery**
★★★ Willa Jean $ *611 O'Keefe Ave. (p 108)*

Best **Upscale Cajun Restaurant in an Old House**
★★★ Brigtsen's $$ *723 Dante St. (p 99)*

Best **Balcony Dining**
★★ Tableau $$$ *675 St. Peter St. (p 108)*

Most **Romantic**
★★★ Upperline $$ *1413 Upperline St. (p 108)*

Best **Breakfast**
★★★ Elizabeth's $$ *601 Gallier St. (p 102)*

Best **Neighba'hood Italian**
★★ Liuzza's $ *3636 Bienville St. (p 105)*

Best **Po' Boy**
★★★ Parkway Bakery $ *538 Hagan Ave. (p 106)*

Best **Place to Find Locals**
★ Verti Marte $ *1201 Royal St. (p 108)*

Best **Expense Account Blowout**
★★★ Restaurant August $$$ *301 Tchoupitoulas St. (p 106)*

Best **All-Around New Orleans Dining Experience** ★★★ Commander's Palace $$$ *1403 Washington Ave. (p 100)*

Best **Ice Cream**
★★★ The Creole Creamery $ *4924 Prytania St. (p 101)*

Previous page: Chef Tory McPhail at Commander's Palace.

French Quarter Dining

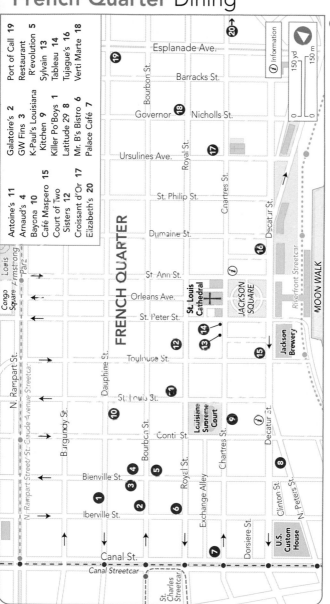

FRENCH QUARTER

Esplanade Ave.

Barracks St.

Bourbon St.

Governor Nicholls St.

Ursulines Ave.

Royal St.

Chartres St.

St. Philip St.

Decatur St.

Dumaine St.

St. Ann St.

Orleans Ave.

St. Louis Cathedral

St. Peter St.

JACKSON SQUARE

Riverfront Streetcar

MOON WALK

Jackson Brewery

Toulouse St.

Dauphine St.

St. Louis St.

Louisiana Supreme Court

Burgundy St.

Conti St.

Bourbon St.

Royal St.

Chartres St.

Decatur St.

Bienville St.

Exchange Alley

Clinton St.

N. Peter St.

Iberville St.

Dorsiere St.

U.S. Custom House

Canal St.

Canal Streetcar

St. Charles Streetcar

N. Rampart St.

N. Rampart Street/ St. Claude Avenue Streetcar

Louis Armstrong Park

Congo Square

Information

150 yd
150 m

Central Business District Dining

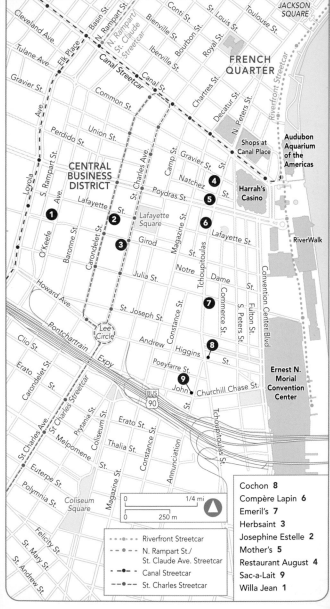

Cochon **8**
Compère Lapin **6**
Emeril's **7**
Herbsaint **3**
Josephine Estelle **2**
Mother's **5**
Restaurant August **4**
Sac-a-Lait **9**
Willa Jean **1**

Riverfront Streetcar
N. Rampart St./
St. Claude Ave. Streetcar
Canal Streetcar
St. Charles Streetcar

Uptown Dining

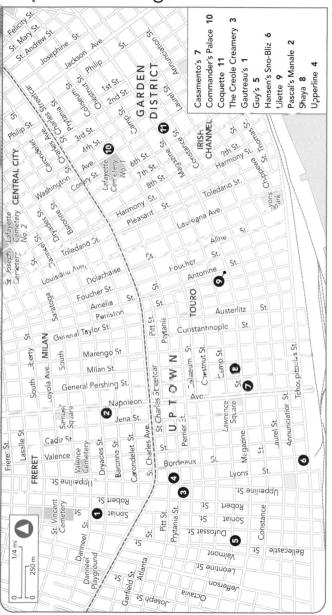

Casamento's 7
Commander's Palace 10
Coquette 11
The Creole Creamery 3
Gautreau's 1
Guy's 5
Hansen's Sno-Bliz 6
Lilette 9
Pascal's Manale 2
Shaya 8
Upperline 4

Carrollton/Mid-City Dining

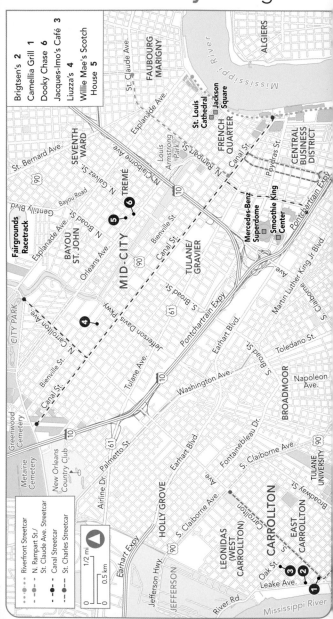

Brigtsen's **2**
Camellia Grill **1**
Dooky Chase **6**
Jacques-Imo's Café **3**
Liuzza's **4**
Willie Mae's Scotch House **5**

Riverfront Streetcar
N. Rampart St./ St. Claude Ave. Streetcar
Canal Streetcar
St. Charles Streetcar

0   1/2 mi
0   0.5 km

Dining A to Z

★★ **Antoine's** FRENCH QUARTER *FRENCH/CREOLE* The oldest restaurant in the city (since 1840—and still run by the same family), Antoine's is one of New Orleans's most lauded and popular upscale establishments. It's all white tablecloths and doting waiters—what's not to love? Start with oysters Rockefeller (invented here) and finish with the flashy, flaming baked Alaska; you can't go wrong with anything in between. Be sure to take a tour, too. *713 St. Louis St.* ☎ *504/581-4422. www.antoines. com. Reservations recommended. No sandals or T-shirts; collared shirts for men. Entrees $27–$48. AE, DC, MC, V. Lunch & dinner Mon–Sat, brunch Sun. Map p 96.*

★★ **Arnaud's** FRENCH QUARTER *CREOLE* Old New Orleans culture haunts you like a splendid specter here, from the moody antique lighting to the dark, butter-rich sauces. Expect traditional crab cakes and shrimp Creole; fantastic fish dishes and solid steaks. Fire up dessert with tableside bananas foster; then venture upstairs for a peek at founder Germaine Wells's early-20th-century haute Carnival couture Worth it. *813 Bienville St.* ☎ *504/ 523-5433. www.arnaudsrestaurant. com. Reservations recommended. Business casual. Entrees $27–$42. AE, DC, DISC, MC, V. Dinner nightly, jazz brunch Sun. Map p 95.*

★★★ **Bayona** FRENCH QUARTER *INTERNATIONAL* A vanguard of modern New Orleans cuisines, chef-owner Susan Spicer serves palate-tempting, international-inflected cuisine in a 200-year-old Creole cottage—one of the city's most romantic spots. Sweetbreads with lemon caper butter are a signature dish; rabbit preparations are

Chef Frank Brigtsen.

consistent standouts as are the vegetarian options. *430 Dauphine St.* ☎ *504/525-4455. www.bayona. com. Reservations required for dinner. Entrees $29–$36. AE, DC, DISC, MC, V. Lunch Wed–Sat, dinner Mon–Sat. Map p 95.*

★★★ **Brigtsen's** CARROLLTON *CREOLE/ACADIAN* The moment you step inside this tucked-away, 19th-century Victorian cottage, hostess Marna Brigtsen will make you feel at home. Chef Frank Brigtsen insists on fresh, seasonal, local ingredients, and the flavor profiles of his traditional-but-refined preparations are flawless. When available, order the mile-high seafood platter. *723 Dante St.* ☎ *504/861-7610. www.brigtsens.com. Reservations required. Entrees $21–$34. AE, DC, MC, V. Dinner Tues–Sat. Map p 98.*

★ **kids Café Maspero** FRENCH QUARTER *SANDWICHES/ SEAFOOD* An extensive menu with plenty of familiar items, good prices, decent food, and a big room make this a solid choice for families and just about everyone

The Best Dining

(except the most demanding gourmands). *601 Decatur St.* ☎ *504/523-6250. www.cafemaspero.com. Entrees $4.25–$9. AE, DISC, MC, V. Lunch & dinner daily. Map p 95.*

★★ kids Camellia Grill

UPTOWN *DINER* Take the St. Charles Avenue streetcar until the Riverbend, where it makes a big right turn. Hop off. Head to white columned building. Sit at the counter with your linen napkin, banter with the feisty waiters, order a simple burger or omelet, finish with a slice of grilled chocolate pecan pie, a la mode. Perfection. *626 S. Carrollton Ave.* ☎ *504/309-2679. All items under $15. MC, V. Breakfast, lunch & dinner daily. Map p 98.*

★★★ Casamento's MAGAZINE

STREET *SEAFOOD* The lines might be longer at Acme Oyster House in the French Quarter (724 Iberville St.), but we're sending you Uptown for the best bivalves and the best shucker in the best, old school, tile-walled setting. Get 'em raw, chargrilled, and in the fried oyster loaf. *4330 Magazine St www.casamentosrestaurant.com.* ☎ *504/895-9761. $9–$25, No credit cards. Lunch Tues–Sat, dinner Thurs–Sat. Closed late May to early Sept and major holidays. Map p 97.*

★★ Cochon CENTRAL BUSINESS

DISTRICT *CONTEMPORARY CAJUN* Rustic Cajun cuisine is amped up with a modern hand at this mega-popular, multi-award winner. We can vouch for pretty much all the small plates and boucherie. Though pork is its forte, the soul-warming skillet-baked rabbit and dumplings is also stupendous. *930 Tchoupitoulas St.* ☎ *504/588-2123. www.cochon restaurant.com. Reservations strongly recommended. Small plates $8–14, main courses $16–20. AE, DC, DISC, MC, V. Lunch & dinner Mon–Sat. Map p 96.*

★★★ Commander's Palace

GARDEN DISTRICT *CREOLE* Still the ultimate, all-around New Orleans dining experience, in our opinion. Stellar service; cuisine that references the Creole past and superbly, deliciously brings it into the present (legendary chefs Paul Prudhomme and Emeril Lagasse got their starts here); elegant but playful decor; a massive wine cellar; and prix-fixe options that won't break the bank. But it's the welcoming, unstuffy atmosphere that perennially nets Commander's our top spot, and that of tourists and locals alike. *1403 Washington Ave.* ☎ *504/899-8221. www.commanders palace.com. Upscale dress, jackets preferred at dinner; no shorts or T-shirts. Entrees $36–$45, brunch $27–$32. AE, DC, DISC, MC, V. Lunch Mon–Fri, dinner nightly, jazz brunch Sat–Sun. Map p 97.*

★★★ Compere Lapin

CENTRAL BUSINESS DISTRICT *MODERN SOUTHERN* Nina Compton, a runner-up and fan favorite of the Food Network's *Top Chef*, melds a touch of her Caribbean roots with farm-fresh local ingredients and classic French techniques, resulting in clean, crisp creativity on the palate. Killer cocktails too. *535 Tchoupitoulas St.* ☎ *504/599-2119. www.comperelapin.com. Entrees $24–$32. AE, MC, V. Lunch & dinner daily. Map p 96.*

★★★ Coquette MAGAZINE

STREET *BISTRO* Coquette is smart and polished in both style and cuisine, and chef/owner Michael Stoltzfus' culinary creativity keeps it ever fresh. His dedication to ingredient perfection, and the top talent heading the bar and pastry programs, make Coquette a favorite. Spring for the tasting menu if you can. *2800 Magazine St.* ☎ *504/265-0421. www. coquettenola.com. Reservations*

Lunch at Compère Lapin.

highly recommended. Friday 3-course lunch $30; 5-course blind tasting $70; dinner entrees $25–32. AE, DC, DISC, MC, V. Lunch Fri, dinner daily, Sat & Sun brunch. Map p 96.

kids Court of Two Sisters
FRENCH QUARTER *CREOLE* The exposed brick, soothing fountain, and jazz music add up to a stronger impression than the food, which includes takes on Creole-style fish, fowl, and beef. Reasonably priced children's menu available. *613 Royal St.* ☎ *504/522-7261.* www.courtof twosisters.com. *Reservations recommended. Entrees $25–$35, Jazz brunch $29. AE, DC, DISC, MC, V. Brunch & dinner daily. Map p 95.*

★★★ kids The Creole Creamery
UPTOWN *DESSERT* This neighborhood ice cream parlor looks like a throwback to the 1950s but boasts traditionally and totally modern taste combinations, like lavender honey, Chinese five-spice, and earl grey. If you can't decide, choose a sampler with four or six mini-scoops. *4924 Prytania St.* ☎ *504/894-8680.* www.creolecreamery.com. *Everything under $10. No credit cards. Sun–Thurs noon–10pm, Fri–Sat noon–11pm. Map p 97.*

★★ Croissant d'Or
FRENCH QUARTER *SANDWICHES/PASTRIES* A quiet French bakery in which to sip delicious iced coffee and munch flaky chocolate croissants, mini apple tarts, quiche, and crunchy tuna-salad sandwiches. *617 Ursulines Ave.* ☎ *504/524-4663.* www.croissantdornula.com. *Entrees $8 and under. MC, V. Breakfast & lunch Wed–Mon. Map p 95.*

★ Dooky Chase
TREME *CREOLE/SOUL FOOD* Upscale, soul food from renowned, history-making nonagenarian chef-matriarch Leah Chase and grandson Edgar "Dook" Chase IV, a Le Cordon Bleu grad. *2301 Orleans Ave.* ☎ *504/821-0600.* www.dookychase restaurant.com. *Entrees $9–$26. No*

There's a flavor for everyone at the Creole Creamery.

Old-fashioned calas with maple syrup at Elizabeth's in Bywater.

credit cards. Lunch Tues–Fri dine in or take out, dinner Fri. Map p 98.

★★★ kids **Elizabeth's** BYWA-TER *BREAKFAST/CREOLE* It's out of the way, but one taste of the sweet, crispy praline bacon, and you'll understand why the location is no obstacle. *601 Gallier St. ☎ 504/944-9272. www.elizabeths restaurantnola.com. Entrees $8.50–$17. MC, V. Breakfast & lunch daily, dinner Mon–Sat. Map p 95.*

★★★ **Emeril's** CENTRAL BUSINESS DISTRICT *CREOLE/NEW AMERICAN* Who doesn't know the "Bam" man? Don't dismiss his namesake restaurant due to his mega-star status. Instead, indulge. There's a reason he got so

famous—and it's on proud, delectable display on every plate at this flagship, fine-dining establishment, where the food and service are kicked up more than a notch. *800 Tchoupitoulas St. ☎ 504/528-9393. www.emerilsrestaurants.com/emerils-new-orleans. Reservations recommended. Entrees $24–$60; degustation menu available (arranged in advance). AE, DC, DISC, MC, V. Lunch Mon–Fri, dinner daily. Map p 96.*

★★ **Galatoire's** FRENCH QUARTER *FRENCH* Grab Tennessee Williams's table (in the main window, in front of the word "Restaurant") and prepare to be satiated by extravagant multicourse French meals prepared from recipes that have been in the family since 1905 and served generations, especially for the ritualistic Friday lunch. *209 Bourbon St. ☎ 504/525-2021. www.galatoires.com. Reservations accepted for 2nd-floor dining room only. Jackets required for dinner and on Sun. Entrees $21–$42. AE, DC, DISC, MC, V. Lunch & dinner Tues–Sun. Map p 95.*

★★ **Gautreau's** UPTOWN *FRENCH* The flickering candlelight, Parisian-style *trompe l'oeil* on

Emeril's dining room.

French cuisine at Galatoire's.

the walls, and tin ceiling set a romantic mood in this soigné, brilliantly converted neighborhood drugstore. (The original antique apothecary cases now display wine and liquor.) The inventive, modern menu changes seasonally, but the seafood options never disappoint. *1728 Soniat St.* ☎ *504/899-7397. www.gautreausrestaurant.com. Reservations recommended. Business casual. Entrees $25–$35. AE, MC, V. Dinner Mon–Sat. Map p 97.*

★★ **Guy's** UPTOWN *SAND-WICHES* Owner Marvin Matherne will personally make you the best grilled-shrimp po'boy you've ever had. Be sure to grab lots of napkins because that fresh French bread can soak up only so much buttery juice. *5259 Magazine St.* ☎ *504/891-5025. Sandwiches $6.50–$12. No credit cards. Lunch Mon–Sat. Map p 97.*

★★★ **GW Fins** FRENCH QUARTER *SEAFOOD* This shrine to seafood is a grown-up restaurant, to be sure, where preparations are stylish but never upstage the star: bratty fresh fish from the Gulf and far afield. You can't miss with the signature "scalibut" (thin-sliced scallop "scales" atop grilled halibut) or lobster risotto, complemented by a smart wine list. End with the

pretzel-crusted salty malty ice cream pie. *808 Bienville St.* ☎ *504/581-3467. www.gwfins.com. Reservations recommended. Collared shirts for men; better jeans; no shorts or flip-flops. Entrees $21–38. AE, DISC, MC, V. Dinner daily. Map p 95.*

★★ **kids Hansen's Sno-Bliz** UPTOWN *DESSERT* Ernest and Mary Hansen founded this family favorite back in 1939; their granddaughter Ashley continues to run it today. Ernest's snowball machine invention creates such finely shaved ice that it's like eating snowflakes. While waiting in line, check out the fun wall of photos of past patrons. *4801 Tchoupitoulas St.* ☎ *504/891-9788. www.snobliz.com. Cash only. Tues–Sun 1–7pm, open spring–fall. Map p 97.*

★★★ **Herbsaint** CENTRAL BUSINESS DISTRICT *FRENCH/NEW AMERICAN* Chef-owner Donald Link, a local culinary demigod (with good reason) offers hearty but sophisticated Southern comfort food in an upscale bistro setting. *701 St. Charles Ave.* ☎ *504/524-4114. www.herbsaint.com. Reservations recommended. Entrees $26–$34 AE, DC, DISC, MC, V. Lunch Mon–Fri, dinner Mon–Sat. Map p 96.*

★★ **Jacques-Imo's Café** CARROLLTON *CREOLE/SOUL FOOD* Enjoy your stuffed pork chop or fried chicken seated in the

Fish dinner at Gautreau's.

Pineapple and necta-cream Sno-Bliz from Hansen's Sno-Bliz.

truck parked outside and be the envy of all. It's funky and fun inside, too. *8324 Oak St.* ☎ *504/861-0886. www.jacques-imos.com. Reservations required for parties of 5 or more. Entrees $19–$37. AE, DC, DISC, MC, V. Dinner Mon–Sat. Map p 98.*

★★ **Josephine Estelle** CEN-TRAL BUSINESS DISTRICT *ITAL-IAN* Located in the über-hip Ace Hotel, the restaurant is not at all too cool for regular people—and it's superb. Any of the crudo starters are recommended; also do your best to work your way through the entire pasta selection. *600 Caronde-let St.* ☎ *504/930-3070. www. josephineestelle.com. Entrees $14–$35. AE, MC, V. Breakfast, lunch & dinner daily. Map p 96.*

★★ **K-Paul's Louisiana Kitchen** FRENCH QUARTER *CAJUN* Chef-founder Paul Prud-homme's left quite a legacy: his signature blackened redfish, which started the Cajun food craze. It's still delicious, in a po'boy at casual and affordable lunch or at dinner, when white tablecloths and higher prices prevail. *416 Chartres St.* ☎ *504/596-2530. www.kpauls.com. Reservations recommended. Business casual. Entrees $27–$36. AE, DC, DISC, MC, V. Lunch Thurs–Sat, dinner Mon–Sat. Map p 95.*

★★★ **Killer Po'Boys** FRENCH QUARTER *SANDWICHES* It's a pop-up. It's a restaurant. It's so good, it's both. "Little Killer" is per-manently popped in the back of a bar; "Big Killer" has a larger space and menu. Its bun-based boda-ciousness includes a banh mi play: a seared gulf shrimp po'boy with flavors of coriander, lime, and sriracha; and rum and ginger glazed pork belly with lime slaw. The name fits. *www.killerpoboys.com. Big Killer: 219 Dauphine St.;* ☎ *504/462-2731. Wed–Mon 10am–5pm. Little Killer: 811 Conti St. in Erin Rose Bar.* ☎ *504/252-5745. Wed–Mon noon–midnight. Sandwiches $8–13. Cash only. Map p 95.*

Herbsaint dining room.

Dinner in the truck at Jacques-Imo's.

★★★ Latitude 29 FRENCH QUARTER *INTERNATIONAL/POLYNESIAN* Founder Jeff "Beachbum" Berry—who literally wrote the book on Tiki—proves it's more craft than kitsch. His temple to the mid century trend pays reverence through perfect cocktails (teeny umbrellas included) and excellent, updated Polynesian food. Don't skip the riblets. *321 N. Peters St. in the Bienville House Hotel.* ☎ *504/609-3811. www.latitude29nola.com. Entrees $14–$29. AE, DC, DISC, MC, V. Sun–Thurs 3–11pm; Fri–Sat noon–midnight. Map p 95.*

★★ Lilette UPTOWN *CREOLE/FRENCH* Classic French fare meets experimental Creole flair in a highly refined but cozy corner bistro. *3637 Magazine St.* ☎ *504/895-1636. www.liletterestaurant.com. Reservations recommended. Entrees $22–$37. AE, DISC, MC, V. Lunch & dinner Tues–Sat. Map p 97.*

★★ kids Liuzza's MID-CITY *ITALIAN/SANDWICHES/SEAFOOD* Locals have loved the simple comfort food here—including pastas, salads, and sandwiches—since 1947. Massive frosty mugs of Abita beer are a must. *3636 Bienville St.* ☎ *504/482-9120. www.liuzzas.com. Entrees $10–$20. No credit cards. Lunch daily, dinner Tues–Sat. Map p 98.*

★ kids Mother's CENTRAL BUSINESS DISTRICT *BREAKFAST/CREOLE/SANDWICHES* Nothing fancy, just good, greasy Creole diner food, from po'boys to hot plates. *401 Poydras St.* ☎ *504/523-9656. www.mothersrestaurant.net. Entrees $9–$25. AE, DISC, MC, V. Breakfast, lunch & dinner daily. Map p 96.*

★★ Mr. B's Bistro FRENCH QUARTER *CONTEMPORARY CREOLE* A Brennan family favorite among businesspeople and politicians brokering lunchtime deals in the dark wood booths. The

Josephine Estelle in the Ace Hotel.

barbequed shrimp is legendary; crab cakes and Gumbo Ya-Ya are also excellent. *201 Royal St.* ☎ *504/523-2078. www.mrbsbistro. com. Entrees $26–$38. AE, DC, DISC, MC, V. Lunch & dinner Mon–Sat, jazz brunch Sun. Map p 95.*

★★ Palace Café FRENCH QUARTER *CONTEMPORARY CREOLE*

Part of the Brennan family of restaurants, Palace Café offers creative takes on seafood, pork, and seasonal specialties, plus an excellent upstairs floor rum bar. We enjoy the Parisian-style sidewalk tables. For dessert? four words: white chocolate bread pudding. You're welcome. *605 Canal St.* ☎ *504/523-1661. www.palacecafe. com. Entrees $23–$34. AE, DC, DISC, MC, V. Lunch & dinner daily, brunch Sun. Map p 95.*

★★★ Parkway Bakery MID-CITY SANDWICHES

We worried when, after the Obamas dined here, tour buses started rolling in and rows of picnic tables were installed. The lines lengthened but quality didn't suffer at this 100-year-old-plus survivor. Known for jam-packed po'boys like the perfectly fried shrimp, drippingly juicy roast beef, and crisp fried oyster (Mon and Wed only), we're also fond of the reuben and the sides. Don't skip the banana pudding. *538 Hagan Ave.* ☎ *504/482-3047. www. parkwaypoorboys.com Everything under $18. Sandwiches $4–$19. AE, DISC, MC, V. Lunch & dinner Wed–Mon. Map p 96.*

★★★ Pascal's Manale

UPTOWN *ITALIAN/SEAFOOD/ STEAKHOUSE* Order a dozen and josh with Uptown T, the legendary oyster shucker. Then strap on a bib and get the decadent barbecued shrimp (also legendary). *1838 Napoleon Ave.* ☎ *504/895-4877. www. pascalsmanale.com. Reservations*

August's Trout Pontchartrain.

recommended. *Entrees $17–$39. AE, DC, DISC, MC, V. Lunch Mon–Fri, dinner Mon–Sat. Map p 97.*

★ Port of Call FRENCH QUARTER *HAMBURGERS*

The wait may be long but when you're craving an anti-slider (read: huge, juicy burger) and loaded tater, it's worth it. *838 Esplanade Ave.* ☎ *504/523-0120. www.portofcallnola.com. Entrees $12–$27. AE, MC, V. Lunch & dinner daily. Map p 95.*

★★★ Restaurant August

CENTRAL BUSINESS DISTRICT *CONTEMPORARY FRENCH* Executive chef/Food Channel superstar John Besh applies his native Louisiana instincts to graceful, French-based dishes in an elegant, upscale setting. *301 Tchoupitoulas St.* ☎ *504/299-9777. www.restaurantaugust.com. Reservations recommended. Entrees $35–$42. AE, DC, MC, V. Lunch Fri, dinner daily. Map p 96.*

★★ Restaurant R'evolution

FRENCH QUARTER *NEW LOUISIANA* Food world icons John Folse and Rick Tramonto take Creole cuisine in globe-hopping directions keyed to New Orleans' influences with big-league, big-idea, big-ticket dining in a fanciful but refined

setting. Get the deep, dark "Death by Gumbo" with baby quail, and lustrous duck liver mousse. Then its shrimp and grits or the divine tournedos of beef. *777 Bienville St. (in the Royal Sonesta Hotel).* ☎ *504/553-2277. www.revolution nola.com. Reservations recommended. Entrees $33–$52. AE, DC, DISC, MC, V. Lunch Wed–Fri; dinner daily; Sun brunch. Map p 95.*

★★★ **Sac-a-Lait** CENTRAL BUSINESS DISTRICT *MODERN RUSTIC SOUTHERN* Take ideas and ingredients found and honed at hunting and fishing camps. Add imagination. Turn up to 11. This rustic, game-driven cuisine is anything but unpolished, and not for the culinarily cautious, but you will be rewarded. Start at the raw bar; then try the house specialty Lost Fish, and the rich, brimming river gumbo. *1051 Annunciation St.* ☎ *504/324-3658. www.sac-a-lait restaurant.com. Entrees $22–$45. AE, DISC, MC, V. Lunch Fri & Sun; dinner Tues–Sat. Map p 96.*

★★★ **Shaya** UPTOWN *ISRAELI* Who comes to New Orleans and dines on…Israeli food? You, if you're wise (and you can get a reservation). Fresh, modern Mediterranean flavors; silken hummus; and

Butter-poached lobster with sheep's milk ricotta gnocchi at R'evolution.

endless little bowls of mezze (like the signature, peppery *lutenitsa*) might be what garnered Shaya the James Beard award for Best New Restaurant. Or perhaps it's the addictive puffs of pita bread. No, we're sure it's the slow roast lamb shank in a creamy pool of whipped feta. *4213 Magazine St.* ☎ *504/891-4213. www.shayarestaurant.com. Mezze & small plates $9–22, entrees $12–18 lunch; $18–36 dinner. AE, DISC, MC, V. Lunch & dinner daily. Map p 97.*

★★ **Sylvain** FRENCH QUARTER *BISTRO* Darling, delicious Sylvain is set in a thoughtfully renovated carriage house that once belonged to an infamous Storyville madam

Hummus dish at Shaya.

who's said to still hang around. The crostinis, Brussels sprouts, and braised beef cheeks are musts, as are the fine craft cocktails. Dessert can only be the chocolate pot de crème. *625 Chartres St. ☎ 504/265-8123. www.sylvainnola.com. Entrees $19–$28. AE, DC, DISC, MC, V. Lunch Fri–Sun, dinner daily. Map p 95.*

★★ **Tableau** FRENCH QUARTER *MODERN CREOLE* Enjoying a bit of bubbly, a "Grand Royal" quartet of seafood starters, and a crisped crème brulee on Tableau's balcony overlooking Jackson Square is paradise beyond any tropical beach. In cooler climes, go with the sublime bacon-wrapped, rosemary-skewered oysters and juicy Chicken Tableau in Béarnaise sauce. Inside the fancier dining room, the experience honors 1880s New Orleans gastronomy with 21st-century flair. *616 St. Peter St. ☎ 504/934-3463. www.tableaufrenchquarter.com. Entrees $19–$46 dinner, $12–$26 brunch. AE, DC, DISC, MC, V. Breakfast, lunch & dinner daily. Map p 95.*

★ **Tujague's** FRENCH QUARTER *CREOLE* Old-fashioned and set in its ways, what do you expect from a restaurant dating back to 1856? Beef brisket and shrimp rémoulade are signature offerings. *823 Decatur St. ☎ 504/525-8676. www.tujagues.com. Reservations recommended. 6 courses $23–$39. AE, DC, DISC, MC, V. Sat–Sun lunch, dinner nightly. Map p 95.*

★★★ **Upperline** UPTOWN *CREOLE/ECLECTIC* The ambiance is as lovely as owner-hostess JoAnn Clevenger is personally. She makes a point of visiting every table to chat with diners, so do your best to tear yourself away from those fried green tomatoes topped with tangy shrimp rémoulade. *1413 Upperline St. ☎ 504/891-9822. www.upperline.com. Reservations recommended. Entrees $23–$36; 3 course, prix fixe tasting menu $47. AE, DC, MC, V. Dinner Wed–Sun. Map p 97.*

★ **Verti Marte** FRENCH QUARTER *DELI* This deli counter tucked in the back of a corner grocery shop cranks out a vast array of hot and cold take-out foodstuffs 24 hours a day, and delivers to French Quarter hotels. Cheap, tasty, and very handy. *1201 Royal St. ☎ 504/525-4757. Everything under $10. Cash only. Open 24/7. Map p 95.*

★★★ **Willa Jean** CENTRAL BUSINESS DISTRICT *SANDWICHES/BAKERY* When John Besh's pastry chefs opened their own casual restaurant, we went, natch. And then we went back, repeatedly, because everything from the bread up is divine. *611 O'Keefe Ave. ☎ 504/509-7334. www.willajean.com. Breakfast & lunch, everything under $16; dinner entrees $18–$22. AE, DISC, MC. Breakfast, lunch & dinner daily. Map p 96.*

★★ **Willie Mae's Scotch House** TREME/UPTOWN *SOUL FOOD* Quite possibly (and according to umpteen listicles) the best fried chicken. Period. Allow ample wait and frying time, and get the creamy butter as your side *Tremé: 2401 St. Ann St. ☎ 504/822-9503; Mon–Sat 10am–5pm. Uptown: 7457 St. Charles Ave. ☎ 504/417-5424; Mon–Thurs 11am–8pm; Fri–Sat 11am–9pm. www.williemaesnola.com. Everything under $15. AE, DISC, MC. Maps p 96 and 98.* ●

Nightlife Best Bets

Best Burlesque
★★★ One Eyed Jacks, 615 Toulouse St. (p 121)

Best Happy Hour
★★ The Bombay Club, 830 Conti St. (p 119)

Best Dive Bar
★ Snake & Jake's Xmas Club Lounge, 7612 Oak St. (p 116)

Best Late-Late Spot
★ The Dungeon, 738 Toulouse St. (p 115)

Best Gay & Lesbian
★★ Oz, 800 Bourbon St. (p 118)

Best Cajun Dancing
★★★ Mid-City Lanes Rock 'n' Bowl, 3016 S. Carrolton Ave. (p 116)

Best Historic Bar
★★★ Napoleon House, 500 Chartres St. (p 115)

Best Karaoke
★ Cat's Meow, 701 Bourbon St. (p 119)

Best Jazz Club
★★★ Snug Harbor, 626 Frenchmen St. (p 118)

Best Tiki Bar
★★★ Latitude 29, 321 N. Peters St. (p 117)

Best Pioneering Craft Cocktail Bar
★★★ CURE, 4905 Freret St. (p 117)

Best Classic NOLA Bar
★★★ French 75, 813 Bienville St. (p 117)

Best Neighborhood Bar
★★ Pal's, 949 N. Rendon St. (p 116)

Best (Worst) Place for Cheesy, Hangover-Inducing Drunk Fest
Tropical Isle, 600 & 721 Bourbon St. (p 116)

Previous page: A local favorite, Abita Springs beer.
Below: The world-famous Lafitte's Blacksmith Shop.

French Quarter Nightlife

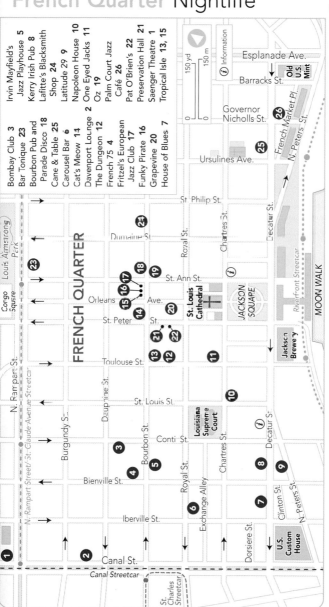

Bombay Club **3**
Bar Tonique **23**
Bourbon Pub and Parade Disco **18**
Cane & Table **25**
Carousel Bar **6**
Cat's Meow **14**
Davenport Lounge **2**
The Dungeon **12**
French 75 **4**
Fritzel's European Jazz Club **17**
Funky Pirate **16**
Grapevine **20**
House of Blues **7**

Irvin Mayfield's Jazz Playhouse **5**
Kerry Irish Pub **8**
Lafitte's Blacksmith Shop **24**
Latitude 29 **9**
Napoleon House **10**
One Eyed Jacks **11**
Oz **19**
Palm Court Jazz Café **26**
Pat O'Brien's **22**
Preservation Hall **21**
Saenger Theatre **1**
Tropical Isle **13, 15**

Uptown Nightlife

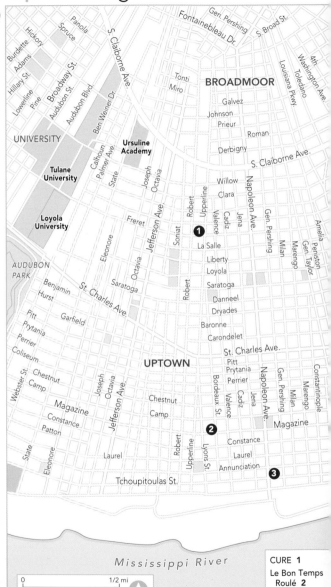

CURE **1**
Le Bon Temps
Roulé **2**
Tipitina's **3**

Central Business District Nightlife

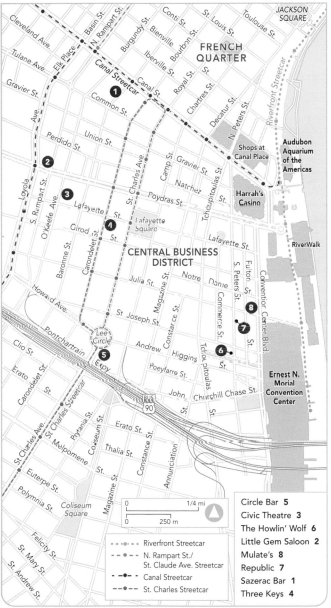

JACKSON SQUARE

FRENCH QUARTER

Shops at Canal Place

Audubon Aquarium of the Americas

Harrah's Casino

RiverWalk

CENTRAL BUSINESS DISTRICT

Lee Circle

Ernest N. Morial Convention Center

Coliseum Square

0	1/4 mi
0	250 m

······•··· Riverfront Streetcar

- - •- - N. Rampart St./
  St. Claude Ave. Streetcar

-·-•- Canal Streetcar

--•-- St. Charles Streetcar

Circle Bar **5**

Civic Theatre **3**

The Howlin' Wolf **6**

Little Gem Saloon **2**

Mulate's **8**

Republic **7**

Sazerac Bar **1**

Three Keys **4**

Carrollton/Mid-City Nightlife

Candlelight Lounge **6**
Chickie Wah Wah **4**
The Maple Leaf **1**
Mid-City Lanes
Rock 'n' Bowl **3**
Pal's Lounge **5**
Snake & Jakes's Xmas
Club Lounge **2**

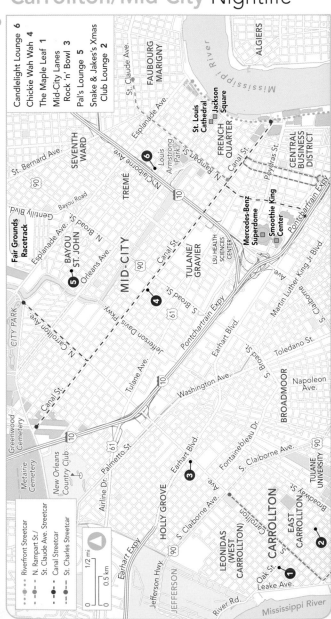

Faubourg Marigny/Bywater
Nightlife

Bacchanal **7**
Blue Nile **6**
d.b.a. **4**
Siberia **1**
Snug Harbor **3**
Spotted Cat
  Music Club **2**
Three Muses **5**

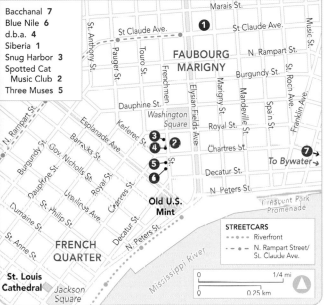

STREETCARS
- - - - - Riverfront
- - • - - N. Rampart Street/
         St. Claude Ave.

0   1/4 mi
0   0.25 km

Nightlife A to Z

Bars, Pubs & Dives
★ The Dungeon FRENCH
QUARTER   Dark and scary in the
good B-movie kind of way, you just
know that bad decisions get made
here regularly (it doesn't even open
till midnight). Claustrophobes
beware. *738 Toulouse St.* ☎ *504/
523-5530. Cover $5. Map p 111.*

★★ Kerry Irish Pub FRENCH
QUARTER   All the essentials are
here: perfect pints of Guinness on
draft; darts and pool; live Irish folk
music; surly bar staff and clientele.
Sláinte. *331 Decatur St.* ☎ *504/527-
5954. No cover. Map p 111.*

★★ Lafitte's Blacksmith Shop
FRENCH QUARTER   Even if it
wasn't the oldest bar (and maybe
building) in the Quarter or a legendary pirate's lair, it'd merit a visit
for the ancient atmosphere. Sip-
ping an ale in the crumbling, cav-
ernlike, candlelit interior is nearly
akin to time traveling (never mind
the anachronistically blaring jukebox). Just step away from the Purple Drank. *941 Bourbon St.* ☎ *504/
593-9761. www.lafittesblacksmith
shop.com. No cover. Map p 111.*

★★★ Napoleon House
FRENCH QUARTER   Do get the
signature, cucumber-fresh Pimm's

Cup at this history-heavy spot with low-key lighting, strong drinks, hot muffulattas, and classical music. *500 Chartres St.* ☎ *504/524-9752. www.napoleonhouse.com. No cover. Map p 111.*

★★ **Pal's Lounge** MID-CITY Locals yammer, dogs wander about, air hockey happens, and some kind of tasty snack is usually available at this true neighborhood hang in the midst of Faubourg St. John. The stellar jukebox and men's room decor add to the lure. *949 N. Rendon St.* ☎ *504/488-7257. No cover. Map p 114.*

★ **Snake & Jake's Xmas Club Lounge** CARROLLTON It's how Webster defined dive bar. Only venture here if you like Christmas decorations year-round, dogs hanging out at their masters' feet, soul and R & B pumping from the jukebox, and really, really dark corners. *7612 Oak St.* ☎ *504/861-2802. www.snakeandjakes.com. No cover. Map p 114.*

Tropical Isle FRENCH QUARTER If drinking slime green-colored rot gut from a plastic, weapon-shaped dispenser is on your bucket list, get an infamous hand grenade here. And that's all we'd better say about that. *600 and 721 Bourbon St.* ☎ *504/529-1702. www.tropicalisle. com. No cover. Map p 111.*

Cajun/Zydeco Venues

★★★ **Mid-City Lanes Rock 'n' Bowl** MID-CITY Bowling and dancing to live Cajun, Zydeco, or rock bands. Need we say more? You don't have to be good at either—a good time is still guaranteed here. Throw a spare, shake a tail feather, rinse, repeat. *3016 S. Carrollton Ave.* ☎ *504/861-1700. www.rocknbowl.com. Shoe rental $1; lane rental $24/hr. Map p 114.*

★ **Mulate's** CENTRAL BUSINESS DISTRICT If you can't travel to Cajun Country, Mulate's brings it to you. Well not quite, but it's the closest the city has to a Cajun dance hall. Thanks to patient instructors and expert live fiddling, all who pass here will pass a good time. *201 Julia St.* ☎ *504/522-1492. www.mulates.com. No cover. Map p 113.*

Concert Venues

★ **Civic Theatre** CENTRAL BUSINESS DISTRICT For years, this 1906, triple-tiered theater stood vacant, save for the exquisite Art Deco chandelier and a flock of pigeons. Now the gracefully restored version hosts diverse acts from John Prine to Slayer to Neutral Milk Hotel. *510 O'Keefe St. www.civicnola.com.* ☎ *504/272-0865. Ticket prices vary according to event. Map p 113.*

★★★ **Saenger Theatre** FRENCH QUARTER Following a gajillion-dollar, post-Katrina renovation, this magnificent 1927 stunner from the movie-house glory days reopened with state-of-the-art technology to host concerts and touring Broadway shows. *1111 Canal St.* ☎ *504/287-0351. www.saengernola. com. Ticket prices vary according to event. Map p 111.*

Craft Cocktail Bars

★★★ **Bar Tonique** FRENCH QUARTER Classic or well-made craft cocktails without pretense amid a good mix of neighborhood locals in a low-key hip room with candles flickering against exposed brick. *820 N. Rampart St.* ☎ *504/ 324-6045. www.bartonique.com. Map p 111.*

★★★ **Cane & Table** FRENCH QUARTER The "sophisticated faded" decor mixes distressed brick with sparkly chandeliers and a gleaming white marble bar top. Rum (made from the cane, get it?) stars, mixed by revered craft

Performance at the Civic Theater.

cocktail revivalists with house-made ingredients and squeezed-to-order juice. Excellent small plates go with. *1113 Decatur St.* ☎ *504/581-1112. www.caneandtablenola.com. Map p 111.*

★★★ **CURE** UPTOWN This mixologist mecca helped instigate the resurgence of both craft cocktails in New Orleans and now-booming Freret Street. The oasis of sleek boasts great small plates and some of the most knowledgeable bar chefs in town. *4905 Freret St. www.curenola.com.* ☎ *504/302-2357. Map p 112.*

★★★ **French 75** FRENCH QUARTER What drinking in New Orleans should be: Classic and classy, in the intimate bar space of one of the Quarter's most venerable restaurants, Arnaud's (p 99). Acclaimed bartender Chris Hannah concocts perfect vintage mixes, namesake champagne cocktails, and originals. Order a side of dreamy soufflé potatoes. Perfection. *813 Bienville St. www.arnauds restaurant.com.* ☎ *504/523-5433. Map p 111.*

★★★ **Latitude 29** FRENCH QUARTER If you think tiki is tacky, think again. When a famed mixologist is behind the concept, it's tasteful and tasty in spades. Drinks, then, are garnished with umbrellas but made with a deft hand, and the proto-Polynesian cuisine is delectable. *321 N. Peters St.* ☎ *504/609-3811. www.latitude29nola.com. Map p 111.*

Dance Clubs

★ **Republic** CENTRAL BUSINESS DISTRICT The under-30 crowd crowds in for EDM, bounce, and occasional live hip-hop shows. The old warehouse space has been

Bar Tonique.

Irvin Mayfield performs at Snug Harbor.

hipped up with chandeliers and pricier drinks. Original wood beams are cool as ceiling struts but mar sightlines as pillars. *828 S. Peters St.* ☎ *504/528-8282. www.republicnola. com. Cover varies. Map p 113.*

Gay/Lesbian Bars

★ **Bourbon Pub and Parade Disco** FRENCH QUARTER One of the country's largest gay clubs, the downstairs bar blares dance music and videos 24/7; upstairs, disco divas in full rainbow regalia get their hustle on every weekend. *801 Bourbon St.* ☎ *504/529-2107. www.bourbonpub.com. Cover $5–$10 weekends only. Map p 111.*

★★ **Oz** FRENCH QUARTER It's all about the bass, the lights, and the hot, highly muscled go-go boys showing off their hip-swiveling moves. Great for people watching or participating. Plenty of straights here too. *800 Bourbon St.* ☎ *504/ 593-9491. www.ozneworeworleans.com. Cover varies. Map p 111.*

Jazz Clubs (Contemporary)

★★ **Irvin Mayfield's Jazz Playhouse** FRENCH QUARTER This swank, draperied, midsize retreat from the Bourbon Street mess showcases über-talented, ethically challenged trumpeter-bandleader Irvin and the ambitious, high-caliber jazz artists he books. Wednesdays featuring the New Orleans Jazz Orchestra and the Friday midnight burlesque show are sure bets. *In the Royal Sonesta Hotel, 300 Bourbon St.* ☎ *504/553-2299. www.irvin mayfield.com. Rarely a cover. One-drink minimum. Map p 111.*

★★★ **Snug Harbor** FAUBOURG MARIGNY The premier modern jazz club in the city, Snug books top local and touring names such as piano patriarch Ellis Marsalis and song stylist Kurt Elling. This is serious, sit-down jazz (food is served in an outer room) but some sightlines are obstructed; arrive early for choice seats. *626 Frenchmen St.* ☎ *504/949-0696. www.snugjazz. com. Cover $15–$40. Map p 115.*

Jazz Clubs (Traditional)

★★ **Fritzel's European Jazz Club** FRENCH QUARTER Squeeze in for some great jazz jams and hope your table-mates remembered the Arrid Extra Dry. Great music and low or no cover makes the tight quarters and pushy door staff worth it. *733 Bourbon St.* ☎ *504/586-4800. www.fritzelsjazz.net. No cover. One-drink minimum per set. Map p 111.*

★★ **Little Gem Saloon** CEN-
TRAL BUSINESS DISTRICT Greats
such as Buddy Bolden and Jelly
Roll Morton played the 1906 Gem.
The sophisticated, restored version
of this jazz motherland books good
local and visiting acts in the brick-
walled, velvet-curtained Ramp
Room, and more casual acts at
happy hour and brunch in the white
tile-floored, first level saloon where
modern Southern food is served.
445 S. Rampart St. www.littlegem
saloon.com. 504/267-4863. Cover
free–$25. Map p 113.

★ **The Palm Court Jazz Café**
FRENCH QUARTER Old-school
jazz in air-conditioned comfort . . .
aah. Pay the cover, stick with drinks,
and pass on the pricey food. 1204
Decatur St. 504/525-0200. www.
palmcourtjazzcafe.com. Cover
$5–$15. Map p 111.

★★★ **Preservation Hall**
FRENCH QUARTER The ancient-
looking building lends the right air
of consecration to this modest but
essential spot for traditional jazz.
The line gets long, it's crowded and
not particularly comfortable, and
there's no bar. The awesomeness is
in the hallowed, intimate atmosphere and the superb musician-
ship. 726 St. Peter St. 888/
946-JAZZ or 504/522-2841. www.
preservationhall.com. Cover $15–$45.
Map p 111.

★★★ **Spotted Cat Music Club**
MARIGNY This teensy, cramped
room has little amplification and less
circulation. We love it. Scrappy,
superb musicians slay it with
refreshed big-band, old timey, gypsy,
hot—well, any kind of swinging jazz
while fleet-footed jitterbuggers join
in (lessons 5pm Wednesdays, FYI).
623 Frenchmen St. No phone. www.
spottedcatmusicclub.com. Cash only.
No cover except special events. 1
drink per set. Tip big! Map p 115.

★★★ **Three Muses** MARIGNY
Small, sophisticated modern lounge
meets classic 1920s saloon. Beautifully balanced, new-timey cocktails +
mouthwatering (quite) small plates +
old-timey tunes + no cover = scant
tables and stools that go fast, so
reserve ahead. 536 Frenchmen St.
www.3musesnola.com. 504/252-
4801. No cover; food/drink minimums.
Tip the band!! Map p 115.

Karaoke

★ **Cat's Meow** FRENCH QUARTER
Karaoke aficionados come from far
and wide to take the mic at this lip
sync mecca, where 3 for 1 drink
specials help loosen the larynx. If
it's your thang, Dream On and
Don't Stop Believing. 701 Bourbon
St. 504/523-2788. www.cats
karaoke.com. Cover $5 under 21, no
cover 21 and over. Map p 111.

Lounges, Swanky Spots &
Piano Bars

★★ **The Bombay Club** FRENCH
QUARTER A massive martini menu
and always reliable piano pros set
this clubby, grown-up lounge apart.
We hope to someday have a reason
to sit at one of the clandestine, cur-
tained booths in the back. In the
Prince Conti Hotel, 830 Conti St.
504/577-2237. www.thebombay
club.com. No cover. Map p 111.

★★ **Carousel Bar** FRENCH
QUARTER There's plenty of soignée sofa seating and fine piano-
based entertainment, but the
classic experience requires a seat at
one of the 25 barstools surrounding
the slooowly spinning carousel
and ordering a Vieux Carré cocktail.
In the storied, immaculate Hotel
Monteleone. 214 Royal St. 504/
523-3341. www.hotelmonteleone.
com. No cover. Map p 111.

★ **Davenport Lounge** FRENCH
QUARTER Swank it up in the
cushy Ritz Carlton room, named for

the silky-voiced, trumpet-playing Jeremy Davenport, who holds court here on weekend eves. Expect tunes from the great American songbook and swooning ladies. *921 Canal St.* ☎ *504/670-2828. www.ritzcarlton.com/neworleans. No cover. Map p 111.*

★ **Pat O'Brien's** FRENCH QUARTER   The world-famous Hurricane, a red rum bomb in a hurricane lamp–style glass, is a dangerous (but required) ritual, but it's the pretty courtyard and flaming fountain that capture our heart. Locals know to opt for the indoor piano bar. *718 St. Peter St.* ☎ *504/525-4823. www.patobriens.com. No cover. Map p 111.*

★★ **The Sazerac Bar** CENTRAL BUSINESS DISTRICT   The posh room in the Roosevelt hotel is named for its signature cocktail. The Ramos Gin Fizz and original 1930s Art Deco murals by artist Paul Ninas also make it worth a visit. *123 Baronne St.* ☎ *504/648-1200. No cover. Map p 113.*

Rock, Blues & Alternative Music Venues

★★ **Blue Nile** MARIGNY   This chill, midsize Frenchmen Street staple has killer sound and no attitude. Local, reggae, and jam bands downstairs; late-night DJs up. *532 Frenchmen St. www.bluenilelive.com.* ☎ *504/948-2583. Map p 115.*

★ **Candlelight Lounge** TREME   One of the last original Faubourg Tremé clubs goes off on Wednesdays night when the incomparable Tremé Brass Band plays. Expect free red beans and rice, cheap fastflowing beer, super-friendly staff, and sweaty dancing. Cab it here. *925 N. Robertson.* ☎ *504/525-4746. Cover $10–$20. Map p 114.*

★★★ **Chickie Wah Wah** MID-CITY   Cool old tin signs lend ambience to the clean, midsize, shotgun-style room in Mid-City, where the best of the local roots, rock, blues, and singer-songwriter acts draw reverent crowds. *2828 Canal St. www.chickiewahwah.com.* ☎ *504/304-4714. Cover $8–$20. Map p 114.*

★ **The Circle Bar** CENTRAL BUSINESS DISTRICT   The 1883 building's quirky, elegant decay suits the laid-back, bar-hugging locals. They wryly debate politics while the Velvets and Dusty feed the idiosyncratic vibe from the jukebox, till some local singer-songwriter takes the alcove stage around 10ish. *1032 St. Charles Ave. at Lee Circle.* ☎ *504/588-2616. www.circlebarneworleans.com. No cover. Map p 113.*

★★★ **d.b.a.** FAUBOURG MARIGNY   We love d.b.a. for its superb beer and spirits selections, chill vibe, Herman Leonard photographs, solid bookings, fair cover charges, and shows that start on time. It's mostly standing-room only and the low stage doesn't help the height-challenged (or the chatter). Catch excellent locals such as crooner John Boutté (his early Saturday set astounds), tight bluesman Walter Washington, and the always

Carousel Bar.

Pat O'Brien's.

entertaining Tin Men. *618 Frenchmen St.* ☎ *504/942-3731. www. dbaneworleans.com. Cover $5–$15. Map p 115.*

Funky Pirate FRENCH QUARTER The XXL attraction here is Chicago-style bluesman "Big" Al Carson, who holds court Tuesday through Saturday. It's popular, sometimes packed, always pirate-y. *727 Bourbon St.* ☎ *504/523-1960. http://thefunkypirate.com. No cover. One-drink minimum. Map p 111.*

House of Blues FRENCH QUARTER No longer the hottest place in town, but holds its own with good sound and sightlines, ersatz folky charm and food, and occasional name bookings. *225 Decatur St.* ☎ *504/310-4999. Cover $10–$50. Map p 111.*

★★ The Howlin' Wolf WAREHOUSE DISTRICT A hand-carved mahogany bar (it once belonged to Al Capone) and magnificent Michalopoulos mural set the stage for occasional mainstream acts such as Alison Krauss, Barenaked Ladies, or Dumpstaphunk in the huge main room and smaller local sets, including the resident Hot 8 brass band, in The Den. *907 S. Peters St.* ☎ *504/529-5844. www.thehowlin wolf.com. Cover varies. Map p 113.*

★ Le Bon Temps Roulé UPTOWN College partiers and regulars couldn't care less about the broken-down surroundings. They're just passing a good time drinking Abita with greasy burgers and jamming, especially if it's Thursday when the Soul Rebels are on. *4801 Magazine St.* ☎ *504/897-3448 or 504/895-8117. No cover. Map p 112.*

★★★ The Maple Leaf CARROLLTON If it's Tuesday when Rebirth Brass Band plays, the tiny patio out back is your respite at this classic club. College kids can run amok, but you'll find their profs here too and a good smattering of tourists listening to great local funk, blues, brass, and rock. *8316 Oak St.* ☎ *504/866-9359. Cover $5–$15. Map p 114.*

★★★ One Eyed Jacks FRENCH QUARTER With its bordello-flavors (swag curtains, red-flocked wallpaper, burlesque), Jack's strikes a funky/retro/hip balance. The '80s nights are legendary, when cool, alternative-leaning local or touring bands play (Surfer Blood, Charles Bradley, Laura Marling, White Denim), the busy front bar and tiered main-room floor are full of cool people. *615 Toulouse St.* ☎ *504/569-8361. www.oneeyed jacks.net. Cover $5–$25. Map p 111.*

Funky Pirate.

The crowd dances to Rebirth Brass Band at the Maple Leaf.

★★ **Siberia** BYWATER A favorite among the pulsing, alternative St. Claude Avenue scene, their sundry bookings span the punk/funk/death metal/trivia/whatev realms. Bonus: fantastic cheap Russian/Creole snacks. *2227 St. Claude Ave.* ☎ *504/265-8855. www.siberianola. com. Cover free–$15. Map p 115.*

★★ **Three Keys** CENTRAL BUSINESS DISTRICT I can't help but admire the adventurous bookings at this newbie, wood-paneled club in the ultrahip, millennial-loving Ace Hotel. But if they're not to your taste, head to the ultrahipper rooftop bar. *600 Carondolet St. in the Ace Hotel.* ☎ *504/941-9191. www. threekeysnola.com. Cover varies. Map p 113.*

★★★ **Tipitina's** UPTOWN Unassuming Tip's—four walls, a buncha bars, a wraparound balcony—is nonetheless *the* New Orleans club: a major musical touchstone and the for local and out-of-town roots, brass, jam, and rock bands, from Wilco to Willie to Wyclef. If you can catch locals like Trombone Shorty, Galactic, or the Meters here, DO. Or dance a la Cajun at the Sunday afternoon Fais Do-do. *501 Napoleon Ave.* ☎ *504/895-8477 or* ☎ *504/897-3943. www.tipitinas.com. Cover $5–$15. Map p 112.*

Wine Bars

★★ **Bacchanal** BYWATER This wine store/bar/tapas restaurant with the sprawling, twinkle-lit backyard and the jazz combo in the corner epitomizes the ramshackle, romantic attraction New Orleans. Locals kick back in plastic chairs, steampunk wine snobs discuss finances, a smattering of out-of-towners enlighten to the tossed-salad ambience. *600 Poland Ave. www.bacchanalwine.com.* ☎ *504/948-9111. Map p 115.*

★ **Grapevine** FRENCH QUARTER The pretty courtyard, good wine, selection, and better-than-expected food make this a destination respite. *720 Orleans St.* ☎ *504/523-1930. www.orleansgrapevine. com. Map p 111.* ●

Performance at Tipitina's.

Arts & Entertainment Best Bets

Best **Classical Class**
★★ Louisiana Philharmonic Orchestra, Orpheum Theatre, *129 Roosevelt Way (p 128)*

Best **High Note**
★★ New Orleans Opera Association, Mahalia Jackson Theater, *1419 Basin St. (p 128)*

Best **Literal Escapist Fare**
★★ Clue Carré, *830 Union St. (p 129)*

Best **Nostalgic Night at the Movies**
★★ Prytania Theatre, *5339 Prytania St. (p 128)*

Best **Place for Dust, Mud or Money to Fly**
★★ Fair Grounds Race Course, *1751 Gentilly Blvd. (p 129)*

Best **Stadium Crowd**
★★★ Mercedes-Benz Superdome, *1 Sugar Bowl Dr. (p 129)*

Best **100 Year-Old Theatre**
★★ Le Petit Théâtre du Vieux Carré, *616 St. Peter St. (p 130)*

Best **Theatrical Culture Shock**
AllWays Lounge, *2240 St. Claude Ave. (p 130)*

A performance on stage at the Mahalia Jackson Theater.

Most **Stunningly Restored Theater**
★★★ Saenger Theatre, *1111 Canal St. (p 131)*

French Quarter A & E

(i) Information
- - • - Riverfront Streetcar
- - • - N. Rampart St /
St. Claude Ave. Streetcar
- - • - Canal Streetcar
- - • - St. Charles Streetcar

St. Louis Cemetery No. 1

Basin St.

Mahalia Jackson Theatre ④

Louis Armstrong Park

Municipal Auditorium

Congo Square

Basin St.

N. Rampart St.

N. Rampart Street/ St. Claude Avenue Streetcar

Burgundy St.

FRENCH QUARTER

Dauphine St.

Ibervile St.

Bienville St.

Bourbon St.

Conti St.

St. Louis St.

Toulouse St.

St. Peter St.

Orleans Ave.

St. Ann St.

Royal St.

Exchange Alley

Louisiana Supreme Court

St. Louis Cathedral

Chartres St.

Dorsiere St.

(i)

JACKSON SQUARE

(i)

US Custom House

Clinton St.

N. Peters St.

Decatur St.

MOON WALK

Riverboat Docks

Riverfront Streetcar

Mississippi River

(i) Information

Woldenberg Riverfront Park

0   150 yd
0   150 m

Audubon Aquarium of the Americas ⑤

Spanish Plaza

Canal St. Ferry

AllWays Lounge **8**
The Broad Theater **2**
Entergy Giant Screen
Theatre **5**
The Fair Grounds
Race Course **3**
Le Petit Théâtre
du Vieux Carré **7**
New Orleans Airlift **9**

New Orleans Opera
Association (Four
Points Sheraton) **6**
New Orleans Opera
Association (Mahalia
Jackson Theatre) **4**
NOCCA **10**
Saenger Theatre **1**
Southern Rep **8**

Central Business District (CBD)
A & E

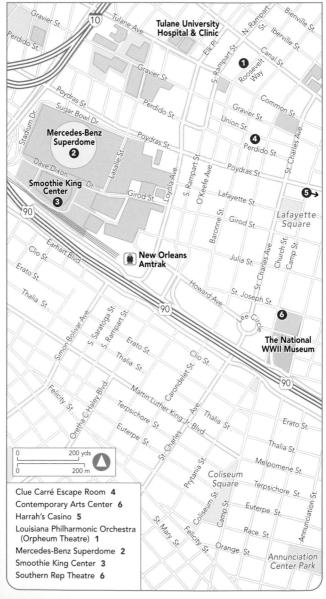

Clue Carré Escape Room **4**

Contemporary Arts Center **6**

Harrah's Casino **5**

Louisiana Philharmonic Orchestra
(Orpheum Theatre) **1**

Mercedes-Benz Superdome **2**

Smoothie King Center **3**

Southern Rep Theatre **6**

Uptown A & E

New Orleans Zephyrs Field **1**

The Prytania Theatre **2**

Zeitgeist Multi-Disciplinary Arts Center **3**

1/4 mi

0.25 km

Arts & Entertainment A to Z

Classical Music, Opera & Dance

★★ Louisiana Philharmonic Orchestra CENTRAL BUSINESS DISTRICT An evening with the LPO in the gloriously restored Orpheum Theatre is one to be savored. Or pack a picnic and chill to the more adventurous repertoire at free, family-friendly concerts in local parks—a favorite locals' tradition. *Orpheum Theatre, 129 Roosevelt Way, plus other venues.* ☎ *504/523-6530. www.lpomusic. com. Tickets $10 and up. Map p 126.*

★★ New Orleans Opera Association FAUBOURG TREME/ FRENCH QUARTER The (arguably) first opera in the U.S. was staged in New Orleans, and the grand tradition still thrives here in terrific, full-scale productions. Or get a taste at free bi-monthly "Opera on Tap" lounge shows at the Four Points by Sheraton Hotel (541 Bourbon St.), where the magnificent French Opera House stood until the fire of 1919. *Mahalia Jackson Theater, 1419 Basin St.* ☎ *504/529-2278.*

www.neworleansopera.org. Ticket prices vary. Map p 125.

Film

★★ The Broad Theater MID-CITY Four screens show mainstream, arty, indie, and specialty fare at this brand spanking new (2016) complex, lovingly built by and for movie fans. Also features occasional live comedy shows, lectures, and such. *636 Broad St.* ☎ *504/218-1008. www.thebroad theater.com. Tickets $8 and up. Map p 125.*

★ Entergy Giant Screen Theatre FRENCH QUARTER Make the steep climb to your seat and prepare to feel like you're actually *in* the movie. It's part of the Audubon Aquarium complex, so it screens nature-oriented films. Like *Star Wars. 1 Canal St.* ☎ *800/774-7394 or 504/581-4629. www.audubon natureinstitute.org/theater. Tickets $5–$12. Map p 125.*

★★ Prytania Theatre UPTOWN This single-screen, neighborhood cinema is the city's

Outside the Mahalia Jackson Theater.

Horse race at the Fair Grounds.

oldest operating theater (with the oldest manager, nonagenarian Mr. René, who may greet you personally), yet it's completely digital, so you get the best of both worlds. Usually shows something new and something old. *5339 Prytania St. ☎ 504/891-2787. www.theprytania. com. Tickets $6–$14. Map p 127.*

Offbeat

★★ Clue Carré Escape Room

CENTRAL BUSINESS DISTRICT Sleuths of all abilities will pass a good time trying to solve their way out of these New Orleans–themed rooms (vampires, check; Voodoo, check). The cryptic and challenging clues are best tackled by small but varied groups. *830 Union St. ☎ 504/667-2583. www.cluecarre. com. Tickets $28. Map p 126.*

★ New Orleans Airlift BYWA-TER

Their output is sporadic, but we've been so entranced by their Music Box installations (sprawling villages of musical instruments created from found materials) that we'll check out anything that this highly creative, DIY-focused artists' collaborative produces. *1031 Piety St. (locations change). www.new orleansairlift.org. Ticket prices vary. Map p 125.*

Sports Venues

★★ Fair Grounds Race Course

MID-CITY The nation's third-oldest horse-racing track has tenaciously overcome fire, hurricanes, world wars, and the Depression—and it's come out ahead. Live races, OTB, and slots attract die-hard gamblers, moneyed socialites, and, on Starlight Racing nights, a new crop of 20-ish types grooving to live music and ponies a'running. Choose the newer, air-conditioned clubhouse or the old-school outdoor grandstands. *1751 Gentilly Blvd. ☎ 504/944-5515. www. fairgroundsracecourse.com. Tickets $10 clubhouse; more for special events. Map p 125.*

★ Harrah's Casino CENTRAL

BUSINESS DISTRICT Got a poker jones? Craps? This is as close as you'll get to Vegas or Atlantic City. And with all types of tables and 1,700 slot machines in 115,000 square feet (10,700 sq. m) of Mardi Gras–themed glitz, it's pretty close. *228 Poydras St. ☎ 800/427-7247. www.caesars.com/harrahs-new-orleans. Map p 126.*

★★★ Mercedes-Benz Super-dome CENTRAL BUSINESS DIS-TRICT

Even if you're not a football fan, if you're in town during a Saints home game, GO. You cannot *not*

A Saints game at the Mercedes-Benz Superdome.

have fun; you also cannot hear for a few days afterward. The venue itself has been vastly enhanced and, amenity-wise, now holds its own with many top sports venues. *1 Sugar Bowl Dr.* ☎ *504/587-3663. www.superdome.com. For Saints tickets, use NFL Ticket Exchange at www.nfl.com. Map p 126.*

★★ New Orleans Zephyrs Field METAIRIE
AAA baseball is good, clean, American fun, and the Zephyrs, farm team for the Miami Marlins, pull out all the cornball stops. Good value and a tidy, comfortable stadium (complete with a swimming pool for rent in the outfield) make this a family fave. *6000 Airline Dr., Metairie.* ☎ *504/734-5155. www.zephyrsbaseball.com. Tickets $6–$15. Map p 127.*

★ Smoothie King Center CENTRAL BUSINESS DISTRICT
The recently amped-up arena is home to the middling but passion-inducing Pelicans (formerly Hornets) NBA team. Some may say it's an apt description for Rihanna and Maroon 5, who've also played there recently. *1501 Dave Dixon Dr.*

☎ *504/587-3822. www.smoothieking center.com or www.nba.com/pelicans. Map p 126.*

Theaters

★ AllWays Lounge BYWATER
Comedy, drag, poetry, erotica, cabaret…it's with good reason that this alternative theater space is called the AllWays. *2240 St. Claude Ave.* ☎ *504/218-5778. www.theallways lounge.net. Map p 125.*

★ Contemporary Arts Center CENTRAL BUSINESS DISTRICT
This social hub attracts fans of modern art, experimental plays, dance productions, concerts, and the occasional film screening. The rooms are small enough that every seat is a good one, although it can be a bit cramped when full. After the show, unwind with some coffee or wine at the Cafe at the CAC. *900 Camp St.* ☎ *504/528-3805. www. cacno.org. Ticket prices vary. Map p 126.*

★★ Le Petit Théâtre du Vieux Carré FRENCH QUARTER
One of the oldest nonprofessional theater troupes in the U.S., Le Petit celebrated its centennial in 2016, most of its years in this charming,

Contemporary Arts Center.

The "Stella" yelling contest at Le Petit Théâtre at the annual Tennessee Williams festival.

recently renovated location off Jackson Square. The company presents classic and contemporary plays, musicals, and experimental fare. *616 St. Peter St.* ☎ *504/522-2081. www.lepetittheatre.com. Tickets $35–$50. Map p 125.*

★★ **NOCCA** BYWATER New Orleans Center for Creative Arts (NOCCA) is the pre-eminent arts school in a city of pre-eminent artists. The caliber of talent is off the charts (grads include Harry Connick, Jr. and Terence Blanchard), making the dance, music, visual art, writing, film, and theater performances well worth the bargain

rates. *2800 Chartres St.* ☎ *504/940-2059. www.nocca.com. Tickets free–$20. Map p 125.*

★★★ **Saenger Theatre** FRENCH QUARTER Opened in 1927 at a cost of $2.5 million—and again in 2013 after a post-Katrina restoration 200 times that—the stunning Saenger is listed on the National Register of Historic Places. The interior resembles a gilded Italian courtyard, complete with hundreds of "starry" ceiling lights. There are few better places to see touring Broadway shows or top acts ranging from Smashing Pumpkins to Diana Ross. *1111 Canal St.*

The interior of the Saenger Theatre.

☎ 504/525-1052. www.saengernola.
com. Map p 125.

★★ Southern Rep Theatre

MULTIPLE LOCATIONS   New and
revival Southern plays are showcased in fine productions by casts
that include both young actors and
experienced local talent. The
troupe operates in multiple venues;
check the website for details.
☎ 504/522-6545. www.southernrep.
com. Tickets $25–$35. Map p 126.

Zeitgeist Multi-Disciplinary Arts Center

UPTOWN   A pio-
neer in the midst of this now-
booming stretch of OC Haley
Boulevard, come here with an open
mind; this is anything but traditional
theater fare. The surroundings and
people-watching are just as fascinating as the experimental shows.
1618 Oretha Castle Haley Blvd.
☎ 504/352-1150. www.zeitgeistinc.
net. Tickets $8–$15. Map p 127. ●

Lodging Best Bets

Most **Luxurious**
★★★ Windsor Court $$$ *300 Gravier St. (p 146)*

Best **Views**
★★★ Loews New Orleans Hotel $$$ *300 Poydras St. (p 143)*

Most **Exclusive Hotel**
★★★ Audubon Cottages $$$ *509 Dauphine St. (p 140)*

Most **Historic**
★★★ Hotel Monteleone $$ *214 Royal St. (p 141)*

Hippest Hotel
★★★ Ace Hotel $$$ *600 Carondelet St. (p 139)*

Best **Moderately Priced Hotel**
★★★ Drury Inn & Suites $$–$$$ *820 Poydras St. (p 141)*

Best **Hidden Gem**
★★★ Jazz Quarters $$ *1129 St. Philip St. (p 142)*

Best **Family Hotel**
★ Homewood Suites $$ *901 Poydras St. (p 141)*

Best **Cheap Bed**
Auberge New Orleans $ *1628 Carondelet St. (p 140)*

Most **Romantic**
★★★ Ashton's $$$ *2023 Esplanade Ave. (p 139)*

Friendliest B&B
★★★ The Chimes $$ *1146 Constantinople St. (p 140)*

Most Over-the Top B&B
★★★ Antebellum Guest House $$ *1333 Esplanade Ave. (p 139)*

Previous page: The lobby bar of the Ace Hotel.
Below: Grand Victorian Bed & Breakfast.

Uptown/Mid-City Lodging

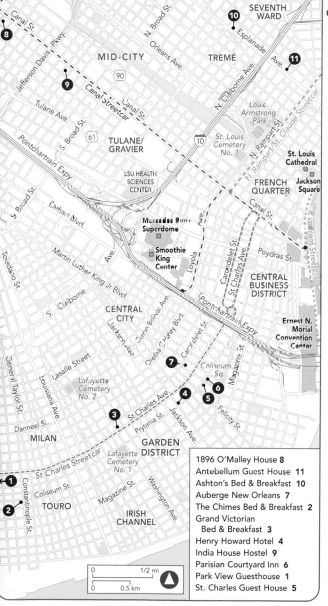

1896 O'Malley House **8**

Antebellum Guest House **11**

Ashton's Bed & Breakfast **10**

Auberge New Orleans **7**

The Chimes Bed & Breakfast **2**

Grand Victorian
  Bed & Breakfast **3**

Henry Howard Hotel **4**

India House Hostel **9**

Parisian Courtyard Inn **6**

Park View Guesthouse **1**

St. Charles Guest House **5**

French Quarter & Faubourg Marigny Lodging

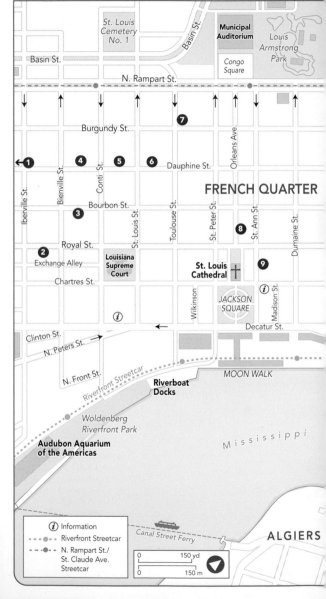

Treme St.

TREMÉ

Ursulines Ave.

Henriette Delille St.

Kerlerec St.

Columbus St.

St. Bernard Ave.

Annette St.

10

11 N. Rampart St.

St.

St. Claude Ave.

N. Rampart Street/ St. Claude Avenue Streetcar

St. Philip St.

Ursulines Ave.

Governor Nicholls St.

Dauphine St.

Barracks St.

14

Kerlerec St.

St. Anthony

N. Rampart St.

Pauger St.

Burgundy St.

Dauphine St.

Bourbon St.

Royal St.

13

12

Chartres St.

Esplanade Ave.

Kerlerec St.

Touro

FAUBOURG
MARIGNY

Frenchmen St.

Royal

Elysian Fields Ave.

St.

Chartres Marigny St.

16→

Decatur St.

French Market Pl.

N. Peters St.

Old
U.S.
Mint

Decatur St.

N. Peters St.

Manderville St.

15

Spain St.

River

Audubon Cottages **6**	Hotel Monteleone **2**	Place d'Armes
Auld Sweet Olive	Hotel Provincial **12**	Hotel **9**
Bed & Breakfast **16**	Jazz Quarters	Ritz-Carlton
B&W Courtyards	Bed & Breakfast **10**	New Orleans **1**
Bed & Breakfast **15**	Maison Dupuy **7**	Royal Sonesta **3**
Bourbon Orleans Hotel **8**	Melrose Mansion **14**	Soniat House **13**
Dauphine Orleans Hotel **5**	New Orleans	
Grenoble House **4**	Courtyard Hotel **11**	

Central Business District Lodging

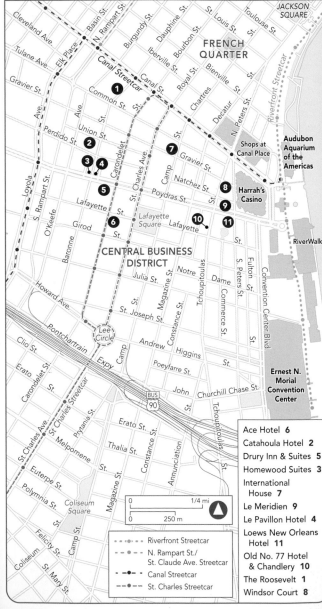

Ace Hotel **6**

Catahoula Hotel **2**

Drury Inn & Suites **5**

Homewood Suites **3**

International
House **7**

Le Meridien **9**

Le Pavillon Hotel **4**

Loews New Orleans
Hotel **11**

Old No. 77 Hotel
& Chandlery **10**

The Roosevelt **1**

Windsor Court **8**

Riverfront Streetcar

N. Rampart St./
St. Claude Ave. Streetcar

Canal Streetcar

St. Charles Streetcar

Lodging A to Z

★★ 1896 O'Malley House

MID-CITY/ESPLANADE   This grand B&B is antiqued but not frilly and just steps from the Canal Street streetcar line. Fine art, stunning woodwork, and a gorgeous fireplace add architectural interest. Host Larry has two friendly golden retrievers. *120 S. Pierce St.* ☎ *504/488-5896. www.1896omalleyhouse.com. 8 units. Doubles $155–$210. Children under 7 not accepted. AE, DISC, MC, V. Map p 135.*

★★★ Ace Hotel CENTRAL

BUSINESS DISTRICT   This hipster bait hotel in a converted Art Deco building should have a soul patch (hello, photo booths and Stumptown coffee). There are record players, vintage vinyl, and ramen packets in the smallish, neutral-tone rooms decorated with nominal, angular furnishings and custom art. But you'll be chillin' with the twenty-somethings in the huge lobby bar, excellent Josephine Estelle (p 104) or Seaworthy restaurant, packed rooftop pool/lounge, or 3 Keys club space. *600 Carondelet St. www.ace-hotel.com/neworleans.* ☎ *504/900-1180. 235 units. Doubles $190–$259. AE, MC, V. Map p 138.*

★★★ Antebellum Guest House MID-CITY/ESPLANADE

Yes, there are antiques everywhere, high ceilings with crystal chandeliers, and elaborate breakfasts. The real difference between this lovely B&B and the city's other historic gems? The hosts who are interesting and interested. You could spend your entire visit chatting with them about New Orleans, art, history, you name it. *1333 Esplanade Ave.* ☎ *504/943-1900. www.antebellumguesthouse.com. 3 units. Doubles $179–$350. AE, MC, V. Map p 135.*

★★★ Ashton's Bed & Breakfast MID-CITY/ESPLANADE   You

may not want to leave your romantic, pastel-walled, antiques-filled room in this antebellum mansion.

Ashton's Bed & Breakfast's Eggs Sardou with Creole creamed spinach, artichoke bottom, poached egg, and hollandaise.

Ceilings are ridiculously high, rooms are spacious, and the sheets silky. But you will, for stellar breakfasts like eggs *cochon au lait.* Plus, the on-site hosts are most congenial. *2023 Esplanade Ave.* ☎ *800/725-4131 or 504/942-7048. www.ashtons bb.com. 8 units. Doubles $209–$279. AE, DC, DISC, MC, V. Map p 135.*

Auberge New Orleans
UPTOWN   This mellow, clean youth hostel has a helpful staff, a decent shared kitchen, and standard-issue metal bunk beds in mixed- and single-gender dorms. *1628 Carondolet St.* ☎ *504/524-5980. www.aubergenola.com. 34 beds. $25–$53. AE, DISC, MC, V. Map p 135.*

★★★ Audubon Cottages
FRENCH QUARTER   A sublime warren of ultra-private, 18th-century cottage apartments, each elegant in its own way. The cottages surround a courtyard and heated pool; it's all attended to by a 24-hour butler. *509 Dauphine St.* ☎ *504/586-1516. www.auduboncottages. com. 7 units. Cottages $299–$999. AE, DISC, MC, V. Map p 136.*

★★ Auld Sweet Olive Bed & Breakfast MARIGNY/BYWATER
Sweet is the operative word for the butter-yellow Creole cottage, from the laziness-inducing wicker porch chairs to the delish breakfast muffins to the airy, custom-painted rooms. It's genuine and unfussy, just like hospitable owner Nancy. *2460 N. Rampart St.* ☎ *877/470-5323 or 504/947-4332. www.sweet olive.com. 5 units. Rooms & suites $145–$300. AE, DC, DISC, MC, V. Map p 137.*

★★ B&W Courtyards Bed & Breakfast FAUBOURG MARIGNY
Most of the distinctive rooms here (they blend West Indian hues with French antiques and Asian touches) open onto a serene courtyard. A killer breakfast starts the day. *2425 Chartres St.* ☎ *800/585-5731 or 504/267-5007. www.bandwcourt yards.com. 6 units. Doubles $169–$235. AE, DISC, MC, V. Map p 137.*

★ kids Bourbon Orleans Hotel
FRENCH QUARTER   Location. Location. Location. And a big pool. This large property has that, plus good service, and even better history. Kids can sleep on pullout sofas in the bi-level suites. *717 Orleans St.* ☎ *866/513-9744 or 504/523-2222. www.bourbonorleans. com. 218 units. Doubles $139–$329. AE, DC, DISC, MC, V. Map p 136.*

★★ Catahoula Hotel CENTRAL BUSINESS DISTRICT   Hiding in plain sight on a side street, this stylish, discreet new boutique hotel is cool but not cold. Small rooms sport comfy Caspar mattresses and historic architectural features, but few amenities (for example, hooks, not closets). Showers that open to the bedroom mean roommates better be very close. But the public spaces are *it:* the so-on-trend pisco bar and Peruvian cafe; the barely lit, clandestine courtyard with a soaring mural of local burlesque star Trixie Minx; and the hip rooftop terrace. Don't overpay. *914 Union St. www.catahoulahotel.com.* ☎ *504/603-2442. 35 units. Doubles $190–$259. AE, MC, V. Map p 138.*

★★★ The Chimes Bed & Breakfast UPTOWN   This gem has no grand airs, just pure charm in a true neighborhood setting. Rooms vary in size but all are tasteful and unfussy, mixing antiques with creature comforts. Lovely, helpful hosts and yummy fresh breakfast pastries. *1146 Constantinople St.* ☎ *504/899-2621. www.chimesneworleans.com. 19 units. Doubles $128–$250. AE, MC, V. Map p 135.*

Guest room at The Chimes Bed & Breakfast.

★★ Dauphine Orleans Hotel

FRENCH QUARTER This labyrinth of vintage rooms, some with private courtyards, others surrounding the popular pool, is quite charming if quirky. Inclusive breakfast and beverages are a bonus. *415 Dauphine St. ☎ 800/521-7111 or 504/586-1800. www.dauphineorleans.com. 111 units. Doubles $139–$269. AE, DC, DISC, MC, V. Map p 136.*

★★★ kids Drury Inn & Suites

CENTRAL BUSINESS DISTRICT The generic decor hides a ton of amenities—free hot breakfast buffet and evening snacks, good-sized pool, helpful staff. Rooms are spacious and pleasant. *820 Poydras St. ☎ 504/529-7800. www.druryhotels.com. 214 units. Doubles $129–$289. AE, DC, DISC, MC, V. Map p 138.*

★★ Grand Victorian Bed & Breakfast

GARDEN DISTRICT This magazine-gorgeous 1893 home is what we picture when we think of a sumptuous, antiques-filled Southern B&B. Some rooms have balconies overlooking the Carnival parade route. *2727 St. Charles Ave. ☎ 800/977-0008 or 504/895-1104. www.gvbb.com. 8*

units. Doubles $165–$235. AE, DISC, MC, V. Map p 135.

★ Homewood Suites

CENTRAL BUSINESS DISTRICT A top choice given all the fringe bennies (hot breakfast buffet, one free dinner, indoor pool, suites with cooking facilities). Homewood boasts a convenient location and fresh, not too chain-like, decor. *901 Poydras St. ☎ 504/581-5599. www.homewoodsuitesneworleans.com. 166 units. Doubles $169–$259. AE, DC, DISC, MC, V. Map p 138.*

★★★ kids Grenoble House

FRENCH QUARTER Full kitchens are in all 17 suites here, a boon to penny pinchers, as is the differing configuration of the rooms (some are large enough for groups). Decor is comfy traditional; guestrooms are set in three historic houses around a courtyard with a heated pool and spa. *323 Dauphine St. ☎ 504/522-1331. www.grenoblehouse.com. 17 units. Doubles $199–$479. AE, DC, MC, V. Map p 136.*

★★ Henry Howard Hotel

LOWER GARDEN DISTRICT A top-to-bottom 2016 renovation turned this stunning, 18 room, 1867 town house with soaring ceilings into a super-chic choice, where sleek, white black blue decor meets classy antiques and unique custom touches. Second-line instruments as artwork and friendly (if limited) amenities like a small parlor bar keep it welcoming. The lower Garden District locale is a bit off the beaten path but convenient to the streetcar line. *2041 Prytania St. www.henryhowardhotel.com. ☎ 504/313-1577. 18 units. Doubles $129–$229. AE, DISC, MC, V. Map p 135.*

★★★ Hotel Monteleone

FRENCH QUARTER One dizzying look at the revolving Carousel Bar and the ornate lobby and you'll

The rooftop pool at the Hotel Monteleone.

know why literary lions such as William Faulkner, Ernest Hemingway, Eudora Welty, and Tennessee Williams stayed here. Rooms range from grand to modest, with traditional furnishings and lots of gilt. Stellar views can be enjoyed from the rooftop pool. *214 Royal St.* ☎ *866/338-4684 or 504/523-3341. www.hotelmonteleone.com. 600 units. Doubles $189–$419. Children under 18 stay free in their parent's room. AE, DC, DISC, MC, V. Map p 136.*

★★ Hotel Provincial FRENCH QUARTER

Run by the Dupepe family since 1969, this luxurious hotel—complete with high ceilings and French and Creole antiques—once housed a Civil War hospital. You'd never know. *1024 Chartres St.*

The sleek, sophisticated lobby of the International House.

☎ *800/535-7922 or 504/581-4995. www.hotelprovincial.com. 92 units. Doubles $119–$279. AE, DC, DISC, MC, V. Map p 137.*

India House Hostel MID-CITY/ESPLANADE

Looking for budget lodging and an instant party? Welcome home. Digs here are funky but not filthy, and staff is friendly. *124 S. Lopez St.* ☎ *504/821-1904. www.indiahousehostel.com. 168 beds. Rooms $20–$90. AE, DC, DISC, MC, V. Map p 135.*

★★ International House CENTRAL BUSINESS DISTRICT

The smallish rooms in this boutique sanctuary are minimalist chic in grays and pale golds, with comfy beds and fab bathrooms—a nice contrast to the city's Victoriana. All that cool, including craft cocktail bar **Loa,** makes it popular with biz types and film crews. *221 Camp St.* ☎ *800/633-5770 or 504/553-9550. www.ih hotel.com. 117 units. Doubles $135–$444. AE, DC, MC, V. Map p 138.*

★★★ Jazz Quarters Bed & Breakfast FRENCH QUARTER

An enclave of entrancing private cottages and a languid tropical garden lie hidden near Armstrong Park. The one- and two-room parlor suites are decorated for comfort with smart, contemporary wares and a smattering of antiques.

1129 St. Philip St. ☎ 800/523-1060 or 504/523-1372. www.jazzquarters.com. 10 units. Rooms & suites $189–$375. AE, DC, DISC, MC, V. Map p 137.

★★ **Le Meridien** CENTRAL BUISINESS DISTRICT   After a $129 million renovation in 2015, Le Meridien rose from the tired remains of the W Hotel with crisp lines and a fresh contemporary feel (read: nouveau *Mad Men*–style furnishings, comfy beds, and plenty of amenities). *333 Poydras St.* ☎ *504/525-9444. www.lemeridienneworleans hotel.com. 410 units. Doubles $139–$319. AE, DC, DISC, MC, V. Map p 138.*

★★ **Le Pavillon Hotel** CENTRAL BUSINESS DISTRICT   Extravagance, thy name is Le Pavillon. The soaring lobby's crystal chandeliers, Oriental rugs, and rich oil paintings serve as the backdrop for signature nightly peanut-butter-and-jelly sandwich service (on a silver platter). The heavily draped rooms are fine, but pale in contrast to the luxe public spaces, updated in 2016. *833 Poydras St.* ☎ *800/535-9095 or 504/581-3111. www.lepavillon.com. 226 units. Doubles $149–$319. AE, DC, DISC, MC, V. Map p 138.*

★★★ **Loews New Orleans Hotel** CENTRAL BUSINESS DISTRICT   We're fans of the crisply contemporary Loews, with its judicious sprinkles of New Orleans flavor and genteel service. The bright, expansive rooms come with local photography, understated furnishings, and sophisticated finishes in a muted palette. *300 Poydras St.* ☎ *866/211-6511 or 504/595-3000. www.loewshotels.com/new-orleans. 285 units. Doubles $199–$439. AE, DISC, MC, V. Map p 138.*

★★ **Maison Dupuy** FRENCH QUARTER   This large hotel in a quiet part of the Quarter (though not far from the action) shines for good service and one of the better pools for a mid-range property (heated year-round). Rooms are decent sized; decor is unremarkable but those facing the large interior courtyard get good light (and views of weddings, not infrequently). *1001 Toulouse St.,* ☎ *504/586-8000. www.maisondupuy.com. 200 units. Doubles $169–$369. AE, DISC, MC, V. Map p 136.*

★★★ **Melrose Mansion** FAUBOURG MARIGNY   Looks can be deceiving. Enter this grandly colonnaded 1854 Victorian Gothic, and

Grand River View King room at Lowes New Orleans.

rather than antiques and brocade, you're met with ultramodern, atonal leather furnishings—a sexy shock to the system. Well-appointed guest rooms range from large to enormous and follow the vibe. Included are breakfast, evening wine and cheese, and snacks. *937 Esplanade Ave.* ☎ *800/650-3323 or 504/944-2255. www.frenchquarterhotelgroup. com. 15 units. Doubles $159–$300. AE, DISC, MC, V. Map p 137.*

★ kids **New Orleans Courtyard Hotel** TREME This inn offers French Quarter proximity at fair rates and simple if pleasantly authentic ambience. We're partial to the carriage house rooms with wood floors, exposed brick, and shutters. *1101 N. Rampart St.* ☎ *504/522-7333. www.nocourtyard. com. 21 units. Doubles $129–$219. AE, DISC, MC, V. Map p 137.*

★★ **Old No. 77 Hotel & Chandlery** CENTRAL BUSINESS DISTRICT This steampunky ex-warehouse kept vestiges of the historic decor and added high style and high speed. Rooms vary widely in natural light (vampiric types: request a windowless one), funkiness, and size—none are larger than medium. To make up for tiny

Suite at Old No. 77 Hotel & Chandlery.

bathrooms and limited amenities, they crushed it out of the hipness park by snagging Compere Lapin restaurant (p 100). *535 Tchoupitoulas St.* ☎ *504/527-5271. www.old77 hotel.com. 167 units. Doubles $94–189. AE, DISC, MC, V. Map p 138.*

★★ **Parisian Courtyard Inn** LOWER GARDEN DISTRICT Hospitality and location are key words here, though the digs in this converted 1846 mansion are by no means slouchy (in fact, they have carved antiques and some boast balconies). Affable Aussie host Tracy will direct you and ply you with afternoon brownies. *1726 Prytania St.* ☎ *504/581-4540. www. theparisiancourtyardinn.com. 8 units. Doubles $145–$235. AE, DISC, MC, V. Map p 135.*

★★ **Park View Guesthouse** UPTOWN For Tulane and Loyola

Inside the Melrose Mansion.

Parisian Courtyard Inn.

visitors, and others staying far uptown, this late-1800s boarding-house with easy streetcar access is a top choice. Decor is Victoriana meets-reproduction, the ample breakfast buffet ranks high, and the front porch is stellar for sitting for a spell. *7004 St. Charles Ave.* ☎ *888/533 0726 or 504/861-7564. www.parkviewguesthouse.com. 550 units. Doubles $169–$349. AE, DC, DISC, MC, V. Map p 135.*

Place d'Armes Hotel FRENCH QUARTER Rooms and décor while perfectly serviceable, are showing their age a bit here. But that keeps prices relatively afford-able (continental breakfast is

included). *625 St. Anne St.* ☎ *888/ 626-5917 or 504/524-4531. www. placedarmes.com. 84 units. Doubles $129–$359. AE, DC, DISC, MC, V. Map p 136.*

★★★ Ritz-Carlton New Orleans FRENCH QUARTER

Expect Ritz-level luxury, food, ser-vice and amenities, including a stel-lar spa and the soignée Davenport Lounge. Room decor leans very tra-ditional, but even the smaller rooms benefit from superb bed-ding. It's all quite gracious and stately. *921 Canal St.* ☎ *800/241-3333 or 504/524-1331. www.ritz carlton.com. 452 units. Doubles $299–$499. AE, DISC, MC, V. Map p 136.*

★★ The Roosevelt CENTRAL

BUSINESS DISTRICT This grandi-ose Waldorf property is fairly regal throughout, but the movie-star glamorous lobby is positively stun-ning and the history and pedigree equally impressive. Sizes and views in the traditional looking rooms vary. Suites are ample but the smallest rooms are too small for what you're probably paying. *123 Baronne St.* ☎ *800/WALDORF or 504/648-1200. www.therooosevelt neworleans.com. 504 units. Doubles $269–$499. AE, DC, DISC, MC, V. Map p 138.*

A luxurious room at the Ritz-Carlton.

Courtyard pool at Royal Sonesta.

★★★ Royal Sonesta FRENCH
QUARTER You might forget you're right on Bourbon Street, what with all the graciousness inside. Rooms are among the more handsomely decorated of those that go for French reproductions. Service is outstanding. And the large courtyard pool is wonderfully welcoming. *300 Bourbon St.* ☎ *800/SONESTA or 504/586-0300. www.sonesta.com/royalneworleans. 518 units. Doubles $199–$429. AE, DC, DISC, MC, V. Map p 136.*

St. Charles Guest House
LOWER GARDEN DISTRICT The three 1890s buildings are humble, funky, slightly crumbling, and not for everyone. Still, if you're a budget traveler (who doesn't demand spic-and-span), you'll appreciate the rare combination of location, value, pool, and offbeat charm. *1748 Prytania St.* ☎ *504/523-6556. www.stcharles guesthouse.com. 26 units. Doubles $45–$105. AE, MC, V. Map p 135.*

★★ Soniat House FRENCH
QUARTER Inside these Creole townhouses lie an oasis of indulgent charm. The staff spoils guests; Frette linens cradle them; and the sweet courtyards, candlelit at night, soothe them. The experience is unobsequiously elegant, romantic, and adult. *1133 Chartres St.* ☎ *800/544-8808 or 504/522-0570. www.soniathouse. com. 31 units. Doubles $195–$325. Children under 10 not permitted. AE, MC, V. Map p 137.*

★★★ Windsor Court CENTRAL
BUSINESS DISTRICT There's a kind of hush at this ultra-fine hotel, for decades at the center of NOLA high society. Everything is serene and mannerly from the proper high tea, to the hallway galleries of fine art to the high end **Grill Room.** The city's indisputably best spa is also here. *300 Gravier St.* ☎ *800/928-7898 or 504/523-6000. www.windsor courthotel.com. 322 units. Doubles $245–$495. Children 16 and under free in parent's room. AE, DC, DISC, MC, V. Map p 138.* ●

High-end luxury at the Windsor Court hotel.

Cajun Country

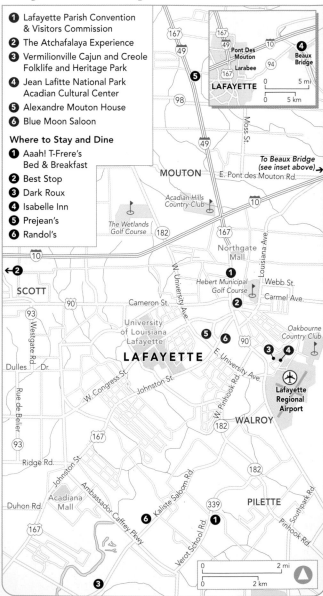

1. Lafayette Parish Convention & Visitors Commission
2. The Atchafalaya Experience
3. Vermilionville Cajun and Creole Folklife and Heritage Park
4. Jean Lafitte National Park Acadian Cultural Center
5. Alexandre Mouton House
6. Blue Moon Saloon

Where to Stay and Dine

1. Aaah! T-Frere's Bed & Breakfast
2. Best Stop
3. Dark Roux
4. Isabelle Inn
5. Prejean's
6. Randol's

Previous page: A group tours the Barataria Preserve outside Lafitte.

When the British overtook the French in Nova Scotia, Canada, the deeply Catholic Acadians (later called "Cajuns") refused to pledge allegiance to the Protestant king. Eventually, British forces brutally uprooted this peaceful, agricultural society. In 1765, 231 of them made their way to this swampy expanse 150 miles west of New Orleans. They rebuilt their lives by farming this inhospitable land, and re-rooted their unique, French-based culture. Owing partly to the popularization of the wonderful food and music, it is now embraced after years of discrimination. START: From New Orleans, head west on Interstate 10. Lafayette, your first stop, is about 135 miles (217km) away, a 2½-hour drive.

A bird in Atchafalaya Basin swamp.

❶ The Lafayette Parish Convention and Visitors Commission.

A good stop for brochures, maps, and friendly info about the city's fascinating combination of Cajun, Caribbean, French, and Spanish influences. *1400 NW Evangeline Thruway, Lafayette.* ☎ 800/346-1958 or 337/232-3737. www.lafayettetravel.com. Weekdays 8:30am–5pm, weekends 9am–5pm.

Head south on NW Evangeline Thruway, turn left at Dudley Avenue, then right at NW Evangeline Thruway/US-167. Turn left on Mudd Avenue/US-90 and turn right on N. Sterling Street (1 mile/1.6km, 3 min.).

❷ The Atchafalaya Experience.

The Atchafalaya Basin is the largest river swamp in the U.S. and home to abundant fish, birds, and other wildlife. Environmentally conscious father–son guides Coerte A. Voorhies, Jr., a semiretired geologist, and Kim B. Voorhies, an avid hunter/fisherman, are virtuoso naturalists who were raised on these bayous and know every inch of this primeval, vital ecosystem. Bring a hat, sunscreen, water, and insect repellent. *338 N. Sterling St., Lafayette.* ☎ 337/277-4726. www.theatchafalayaexperience.com. $50 ages 13 and up, $25 children 8–12, free for 7 and under (1 per family). Call for times and reservations.

Head south on N. Sterling Street then left on E. Simcoe Street. Turn right at Surrey Street then right again at Fisher Road (2 miles/ 3.2km, 7 min.).

A display at Jean Lafitte National Park Acadian Cultural Center.

Alexandre Mouton House.

❸ kids Vermilionville Cajun and Creole Folklife and Heritage Park.

A reconstructed Cajun-Creole settlement where costumed staff and craftspeople demonstrate daily life and musicians jam. It sounds like a kitschy "Cajunland" theme park, but it's actually a good introduction to the culture. *300 Fisher Rd., Lafayette.* ☎ *866/99-BAYOU (992-2968) or 337/233-4077. www.vermilionville.org. Admission $10 adults, $8 seniors, $6 children 6–18, free children 5 and under. Tues–Sun 10am–4pm.*

❹ kids Jean Lafitte National Park Acadian Cultural Center.

Exhibits and digital learning tools show how the Acadian people were exiled from Nova Scotia and settled in the southern Louisiana swamps, where their isolation fostered a unique way of life. *501 Fisher Rd., Lafayette.* ☎ *337/232-0789. www.nps.gov/Jela. Free admission; donations welcome. Tues–Sat 9:30am–4pm.*

Head east on Fisher Road then turn right on Surrey Street. Continue on E. University Avenue. Turn right at Lafayette Street.

❺ Alexandre Mouton House.

This elegant antebellum home on the National Register of Historic Places was originally built for Vermilionville founder Jean Mouton. It now houses the Lafayette Museum's collection of Acadian history and culture. *1122 Lafayette St., Lafayette.* ☎ *337/234-2208. www.lafayettemuseum.com. Admission $5 adults, $3 seniors, $2 students. Tues–Sat 10am–4pm.*

❻ Blue Moon Saloon.

The city's premier live music venue. Cajun, zydeco, and all forms of modern alternative roots music brings in the LSU student body and others. *215 E. Convent St. Lafayette.* ☎ *337/234-2422. www.bluemoon presents.com. Cover $10–$20.*

Blue Moon Saloon.

Where to Stay & Dine

Lodging

★★ Aaah! T-Frere's Bed & Breakfast.
If you have a sense of humor, you'll love this comfortable inn. Former chef Maugie Pastor serves delicious full breakfasts with whimsical names like "Ooh La La, Mardi Gras" while dressed in bright-red silk pajamas. Some rooms are updated with a sleeker look; others are country-Victorian. Try for the Mary Room with the huge antique bed, or the Lafayette. *1905 Verot School Rd., Lafayette.* ☎ *800/984-9347 or 337/984-9347. www.tfrereshouse.com. 0 units. Doubles $135. Rates include breakfast. AE, DC, DISC, MC, V.*

★ kids Isabelle Inn.
Just 15 minutes outside Lafayette, this spacious home is well worth the drive. The Richard Room is beautifully appointed with antiques and offers a gorgeous view from the balcony. I also like the serene cottage feel of the Allison Room. Unlike at most B&Bs, kids are welcome and will love the pool and exploring the garden. *1130 Berard St., Breaux Bridge.* ☎ *337/412-0455. www. isabelleinn.com. 5 units. Doubles $175–$195. AE, MC, V.*

Dining

★★★ Best Stop.
When in Cajun Country, sampling boudin is practically the law. The pork and rice sausage is best eaten straight from the paper wrapper it's served in, accompanied by Zapp's chips and a Barq's root beer. Boudin aficionados debate their favorites, but nearly all put the Best Stop near the top. *615 Hwy. 93, Scott.* ☎ *337/233-5805. www.beststop inscott.com. $. Mon–Sat 6am–8pm, Sun 6am–6pm.*

★★ Dark Roux.
The modern take on fresh local ingredients here shows how Lafayette is advancing the local traditions in a major way. *3524 Kaliste Saloom Rd., Lafayette.* ☎ *337/504-2346. www.darkrouxla. com. Entrees $25–$50. Dinner daily, brunch Fri–Sun.*

★★ kids Prejean's.
All things Cajun greet you as soon as you step inside, including the photo-op-friendly 14-foot (4.2m) taxidermy alligator Big Al, posed in the middle of the swamp-themed dining room. For the Cajun curious, the seafood platter offers all the local specialties on one plate. Live Cajun music nightly. *3480 NE Evangeline Thruway (I-49), Lafayette.* ☎ *337/896-3247. www.prejeans. com. Reservations recommended. Entrees $17–$30. AE, DC, DISC, MC, V. Breakfast, lunch & dinner daily.*

Randol's.
Owner Frank Randol fosters a community spirit here, based on gathering to eat good, simple food and to dance the night away. Indulge in the cheesy, gooey Louisiana crawfish enchiladas, then work off those calories on the dance floor. Locals will show you all the right moves. *2320 Kaliste Saloom Rd., Lafayette.* ☎ *800/962-2586 or 337/981-7080. www.randols. com. Entrees $14–$27. MC, V. Dinner daily.*

Lafitte

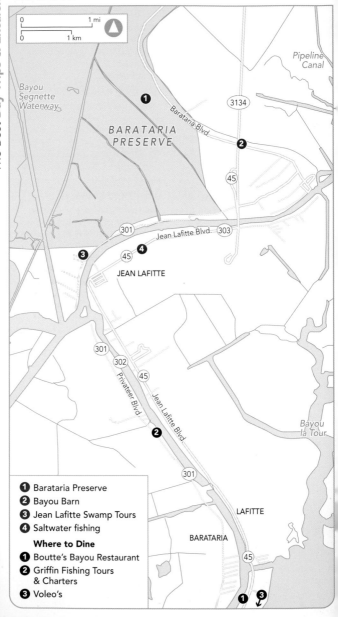

1 Barataria Preserve
2 Bayou Barn
3 Jean Lafitte Swamp Tours
4 Saltwater fishing

Where to Dine
1 Boutte's Bayou Restaurant
2 Griffin Fishing Tours
   & Charters
3 Voleo's

Lafitte is a small, fishing and shrimping town easily accessed from New Orleans. Despite being pummeled by hurricanes and the BP oil spill (and threatened by encroaching development), it's come back, kept its unhurried and comfortable way of life intact, and maintained its natural beauty. It's a welcome escape for explorers and outdoorsfolk. START: **From the New Orleans riverfront, cross the Crescent City Connection over the Mississippi River and get on the Westbank Expressway. At Exit 4B (Barataria Boulevard), turn left onto Barataria Boulevard.**

❶ **The Barataria Preserve.** This untouched preserve offers hiking, fishing, and canoeing along freshwater marshlands and sleepy bayous. There are plenty of prime bird-watching opportunities. Remember mosquito repellent! Visitor center, 6488 Barataria Blvd., Marrero. ☎ 504/589-2133. www.nps. gov/jcla/barataria preserve.htm. Free admission, donations welcome. Trails open daily 7am–dusk, visitor center open Wed–Sun 9:30am–4:30pm.

Head southwest on Barataria Boulevard/LA-301.

❷ **Bayou Barn.** One-stop shopping for canoe, kayak, and pedal boat rentals; a cool drink; and a casual bite to eat. If you're lucky, they'll be having one of their occasional Sunday afternoon fais do do dances when they visit. 7145 Barataria Blvd., Crown Point. ☎ 800/862-2968 or 504/689-2663. www.

bayoubarn.com. Canoe rentals $20–$25/hr. Mon–Fri 10am–5pm, Sat–Sun 10am–8pm.

Head west on Barataria Boulevard/LA-45 N. Take first right onto Leo Kerner Lafitte Parkway/LA-3134 N.

❸ 🧒 **Jean Lafitte Swamp Tours.** Born and bred local tour guides share stories about the legendary pirate Jean Lafitte and the native way of life, while pointing out fish, egrets, nutria, mink, snakes, and, of course, alligators. The more adventurous should opt for the speedy airboat ride. (Yes, they slow down long enough for you to check out the wildlife.) 6601 Leo Kerner Lafitte Parkway, Marrero. ☎ 504/689-4186. www.jeanlafitte swamptour.com. Admission $29 adults, $12 children 4–12, and free children 2 and under. Airboat tour $65–$85 per person ages 8 and up. Call for times and reservations.

The lush Barataria Preserve.

Airboat swamp tour at Jean Lafitte National Park.

Head north on Barataria Boulevard/
LA-301. Turn slightly right at LA-45,
then left to continue on LA-45. Turn
right at LA-3134/LA-45. Turn left at
Jean Lafitte Boulevard/LA-303/
LA-45. Destination will be on right.

❹ **Saltwater fishing.** Captain
Phil Robichaux or a member of his
professional fishing-charter team
can help you locate the lurking redfish and speckled trout. The price
includes tackle, bait, ice, and fish
cleaning. Customers BYO food and
drink. Fishing licenses are required
and can be purchased online or by
phone (www.wlf.louisiana.gov;
☎ 888/765-2602); costs start at $5
per day. Phil also offers overnight
lodging. *1842 Jean Lafitte Blvd.,
Lafitte.* ☎ *504/689-2006. www.fish
withphil.com. $425 per person (dis-
counts for multiple people). Depar-
tures daily 6–6:30am, return
1:30–2:30pm.*

A Cajun Saturday Morning

Two iconic Cajun Country Saturday morning events take place
about 45 minutes from Lafayette. At the Saturday morning jam ses-
sion at **Savoy Music Center** (4413 US Hwy. 190 E.; www.savoymusic
center.com; ☎ 337/457-9563), this nondescript, working music store
(specializing in Marc Savoy's world-renowned, hand-crafted accordi-
ons) becomes the spiritual center of Cajun music. Talented local and
visiting musicians young and old gather to savor this unpretentious,
unparalleled music and culture (endear yourself to the locals by
bringing boudin, donuts, or beer). It runs from 9am to noon, leaving
you enough time to head to the alternate universe known as **Fred's
Lounge** in Mamou, about 20 minutes north (west on U.S. 190, then
right on LA 13; 420 6th St.; ☎ 337/468-5411; Sat 9am–2pm). This is
the other end of the Cajun music spectrum, a small-town bar that for
half a century has hosted Saturday daytime dances (and drinking)
starting at 9am. The hard-working locals let loose as a band plays
waltzes and two-steps. It's a raucous hoot and holler. Join in.

Where to Stay & Dine

Lafitte **is the kind of small town with colorful characters** that you'd think only exist in movies or books. It's definitely worth staying for a spell to mingle with the locals.

Lodging

Griffin Fishing Tours & Charters. Owners James and Rosemary Arcediano provide everything fish-loving families could want. Fish off the private docks or take a guided tour of the brackish Barataria waterways to catch plentiful redfish, speckled trout, bass, and more. Guides will prepare your catch for dockside meals with fellow guests at its own Cajun Cook House. Cabins and camp quarters are rustic but comfy, with plenty of fish and duck decor. Golf and horseshoes are also available. *2629 Privateer Blvd., Barataria.* ☎ *800/741-1340. www.louisianafishingcharters.com. 9 units (4–8 people per cabin/camp). All-inclusive fishing packages $350 per person (full-day fishing tour, accommodations, bait and tackle, meals, snacks, and drinks). AE, DISC, MC, V.*

Dining

kids Boutte's Bayou Restaurant. The scenic drive along the bayou, where you'll see shrimp boats and fishing camps, gives you an idea how important seafood is to this coastal community. Generous portions, friendly waitstaff, and local families make for a relaxed, satisfying meal of shrimp po'boys, gumbo, and fried catfish. *5134 Boutte St., Lafitte.* ☎ *504/689-3889. Entrees $10–$15. AE, MC, V. Lunch Tues–Sun, dinner Thurs–Sun.*

★★ **Voleo's.** You'll probably be the only non-local in this little dive (with surprisingly good cuisine) on a dead-end street, but just take a seat at a checkered table, order Paul Prudhomme protégé David Volion's succulent flounder Lafitte, tap your toes to whatever's playing on the jukebox, and you'll mix right in. *5134 Nunez St., Lafitte.* ☎ *504/689-2482. Entrees $10–$21. MC, V. Lunch & dinner Mon, Wed–Sat.*

A typical meal at Voleo's.

Plantations

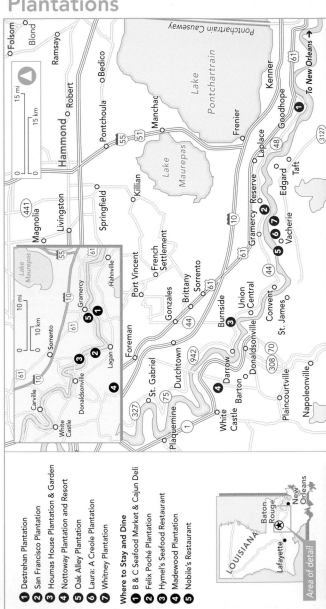

1 Destrehan Plantation
2 San Francisco Plantation
3 Houmas House Plantation & Garden
4 Nottoway Plantation and Resort
5 Oak Alley Plantation
6 Laura: A Creole Plantation
7 Whitney Plantation

Where to Stay and Dine
1 B & C Seafood Market & Cajun Deli
2 Felix Poché Plantation
3 Hymel's Seafood Restaurant
4 Madewood Plantation
5 Nobile's Restaurant

Southern Louisiana's once plentiful plantation homes are now few and far between. The modest, working estates that lined the banks of the Mississippi grew ever grander as did the sugarcane, rice, and cotton industries, especially after the advent of steam-powered river transport. From the 1820s to the beginning of the Civil War, white landowning families relied on slave labor to attain astonishing wealth. Most estates failed after slavery was abolished, unable to sustain themselves—even when subdivided—without the free labor base. Today the homes are a snapshot of an important time in American history, albeit with the omnipresent specter of their shameful past. Most offer optional transportation from New Orleans. START: **From New Orleans, get onto Interstate 10 heading west.**

Some visitors may recognize Destrehan Plantation from the film Interview with the Vampire, *based on the Anne Rice novel.*

❶ Destrehan Plantation. You might recognize this elegant, Greek revival mansion as narrator Louis's (Brad Pitt's) childhood home in *Interview with the Vampire*. Built in 1787 by a free person of color, a meticulous restoration has given it new life, but one area was purposely left untouched so that visitors can better appreciate the humble rawness beneath the public grandeur. ⏱ *45 min. 13034 River Rd., Destrehan.* ☎ *877/453-2095 or 985/764-9315. www.destrehan plantation.org. Admission $20 adults, $15 seniors and military; $7 children 7–17, free children 6 and under. Daily 9am–4pm. Wheelchair accessible.*

❷ San Francisco Plantation. Just picture this country home surrounded by miles of sugar-cane fields. The whimsical "Steamboat Gothic" architecture mimics a ship, but the colorful hues are true to Creole heritage. Inside, look closely

San Francisco Plantation.

Houmas House.

at the faux marble and wood and gaily painted walls, once-popular decorating effects that demonstrated wealth. ⏱ *45 min. 2646 Hwy. 44, Garyville.* ☎ *888/322-1756 or 985/535-2341. www.sanfrancisco plantation.org. Admission $17 adults, $10 students, free children 6 and under; Daily 9:30am–5pm April–Oct; 9am–4pm Nov–March.*

❸ Houmas House Plantation & Garden. Curiously, two homes—one dating back to 1790 and the other to 1840—were joined together under one art-filled roof to make up this enormous estate showcased on 38 acres (15 hectares) of huge live oaks, fragrant magnolias, and perfectly manicured formal gardens. The Bette Davis classic *Hush . . . Hush, Sweet Charlotte* was filmed here. ⏱ *1 hr. 40136 Hwy. 942, Burnside.* ☎ *888/ 323-8314 or 225/473-9380. www. houmashouse.com. Admission $24 adults, $15 children 13–18, $10 children 6–12, free children 5 and under; $10 garden tour only. Daily 9am– 8pm. Cafe and lodging available.*

❹ ★★★ Nottoway Plantation and Resort. Known as the White Castle, Nottoway survived the Civil War because a Union officer had once stayed there as a guest; you can still see scars from shelling on

some of the 22 columns. It's the largest surviving plantation house in the region, with 64 rooms sprawled across 54,000 square feet (5,016 sq. m). Check out the pristine White Ballroom, with its original crystal chandeliers and spooky portrait of a grande dame whose eyes seem to follow you no matter where you go. ⏱ *90 min. 30970 Mississippi River Rd., White Castle.* ☎ *866/LASOUTH*

Portrait of a grande dame in the White Ballroom at the Nottaway Plantation house.

(527-6884) or 225/545-2730. www.
nottoway.com. Admission $20 adults,
$6 children 6–12, free children 5 and
under. Daily 9am–4pm. Cafe and
lodging available.

❺ ★ Oak Alley Plantation.

The famous oak-lined drive nearly
steals the thunder of this quintessential plantation home. Costumed
docents complete the picture-
perfect image, though their robotic
recitations about its history make
you wish you were free to explore
on your own. There are also cottages for overnight stays. ○ 1 hr.
3645 Hwy. 18, Vacherie. ☎ 800/44-
ALLEY (442-5539) or 225/265-2151.
www.oakalleyplantation.com. Admission $20 adults, $7.50 students,
$4.50 children 6–12, free children 5
and under. Mar–Oct daily 9am–5pm;
Nov–Feb Mon–Fri 9am–4:30pm, Sat–
Sun 9am–5pm.

❻ ★★★ Laura: A Creole
Plantation. If you see one plantation, make it this more humble
home and be blown away by the
docents' extensive knowledge and
love for this colorful 200-year-old
Creole estate and its female lin-
eage. The slaves' stories are promi-
nently shared, and the slaves' and
overseer's cabins, which were often
burned so as to "forget" the past,
are still here. ○ 90 min. 2247 Hwy.
18, Vacherie. ☎ 888/799-7690 or
225/265-7690. www.lauraplantation.
com. Admission $20 adults, $6 children 6–17, free children 5 and under.
Daily 10am–4pm.

❼ ★★★ Whitney Plantation.
Dedicated to a frank and thorough
history of slavery as told from the
perspective of the enslaved, visitors
move through somber memorials
(including those of hundreds of
children), resonant tributes, and
shocking remnants such as the
crude iron cage of a jail. Not everything is original (much was razed
before this recently reopened

A guide at Oak Alley, the quintessential
southern plantation home.

(2014) estate was rebuilt, but it's all
harshly authentic, haunting, and
vital. ○ 90 min. 5099 Highway 18,
Wallace. www.whitneyplantation.
com. ☎ 225/265-3300. Admission
$22 adults; $15 seniors, students,
active military; free for children 12
and under. Wed–Mon 9:30am–
4:30pm. Tours hourly. Closed Jan 1,
Mardi Gras Day, July 4, Thanksgiving
Day, Dec 25.

Laura Plantation outbuildings.

Where to Stay & Dine

For the best perspective on the plantation era, see one of the grand estates, a more modest home, and the Whitney. All of that is more doable with an overnight stay.

Lodging

kids Felix Poché Plantation. This 1870 country Victorian home offers a shady porch with river breezes, a French Quarter–style pool, and 22 acres (8.8 hectares) to explore. The private cottages are nice but plain; stay in the main house instead if you prefer richer surroundings. Children are welcome. *6554 Hwy. 44 (River Rd.), Convent.* ☎ *225/562-7728. www.pocheplantation.com. 8 units. Doubles $69–$249. AE, DISC, MC, V.*

★ **Madewood Plantation.** Madewood was originally built by a man who wanted to outshine his brother, but he died of yellow fever before it was finished. Current owners have completely rebuilt the Greek revival masterpiece, including stunning bed and breakfast accommodations. *4250 Hwy. 308, Napoleonville.* ☎ *985/369-7151. www.madewood.com. Doubles $229–$298. DISC, MC, V.*

★★★ **Nottoway Plantation.** Stay the night in this supposed haunted mansion, and you may encounter the spirit of a young, auburn-haired woman in the girls' wing who resembles original owner John Randolph's youngest daughter, Julia Marceline. The master bedroom boasts the Randolphs' original furniture, including a hand-carved rosewood poster bed. Supposedly valuables were hidden in its hollow posts during the Civil War. A newly constructed replica carriage house and cottages are also available with modern amenities. *30970 Mississippi River Rd., White Castle.* ☎ *866/LASOUTH (527-6884) or 225/545-2730. www.nottoway.com. 13 units. Doubles $190–$360. AE, DISC, MC, V.*

Dining

B & C Seafood Market & Cajun Deli. This family-owned and operated joint is near Laura and Oak Alley. Order the seafood platter, filled with shrimp, oysters, catfish, and crawfish; save room for the bread pudding with sticky sweet rum sauce. *2155 Hwy. 18, Vacherie.* ☎ *225/265-8356. $. MC, V. Mon–Fri 11am–4:30pm.*

★★ **kids Hymel's Seafood Restaurant.** Owned and operated by the same family for more than 70 years, Hymel's is renowned for its fresh seafood; SeaSpud potato (topped with real lump crab meat, boiled shrimp, and cheese); and casual, family-friendly atmosphere. *8740 Hwy. 44, Convent.* ☎ *225/562-9910. www.hymelseafood.com. Entrees $10–$30. MC, V. Lunch Tues–Sun, dinner Thurs–Sun.*

★★ **Nobile's Restaurant.** The building and dining rooms seep history, and the food, featuring local seafood and specialties—like rich smothered cabbage with pork chops—is a step up (but still casual). *2082 W. Main St., Lutcher.* ☎ *225/869-8900. www.nobilesrestaurant.com. Entrees $10–$25. MC, V. Lunch & dinner daily.* ●

Madewood Plantation dining room.

The **Savvy Traveler**

Before You Go

Tourist Offices

New Orleans French Quarter: Visitor Information Center, 529 St. Ann St., New Orleans, LA 70116. ☎ 504/568-5661. Vieux Carré Police Station, 334 Royal St. ☎ 504/658-6080.

New Orleans Uptown: New Orleans Metropolitan Convention and Visitors Bureau, 2020 St. Charles Ave., New Orleans, LA 70130. ☎ 800/672-6124 or 504/566-5011; www.neworleanscvb.com. The New Orleans Multicultural Tourism Network also operates out of the same location (☎ 504/523-5652; www.soulofneworleans.com). Note that there are many other "Tour Information" storefronts, offices, and kiosks around town, but they are for-profit businesses that sell tours.

The Best Times to Go

Traditional seasons don't exist in southern Louisiana. (A favorite T-shirt shows icons for Mardi Gras, crawfish, sno-balls, and football to represent winter, spring, summer, and fall.) Truth is, New Orleans offers two extremes: a hot, humid summer (Apr–Nov) and a relatively mild winter (Dec–Mar).

Late June through mid-September can be miserably hot and humid and should be avoided. That said, there are hotel and other bargains, and it's pretty easy to get reservations anywhere. Whether the savings are worth it depends on your personal heat-tolerance level. Early spring and late autumn are our favorite times, and the holiday season is pretty magical (winter temps can be chilly, but rarely dip below freezing).

Hurricane season runs June 1 through November 30, and although named storms are rare, your average tropical thunderstorm is pretty common, so plan accordingly. In fact, rain is possible any time of year. Crowds swell during big festivals, sports events, conventions, and Mardi Gras, of course, and as demand increases, so do prices. So it's worth checking to see what will be happening in town before confirming your travel dates.

Festivals and Special Events

JANUARY. The **Allstate Sugar Bowl Classic** (☎ 504/828-2440; www.allstatesugarbowl.org) attracts die-hard college football fans from all over the country.

FEBRUARY. On **Mardi Gras day** (☎ 800/672-6124 or 504/566-5011; www.mardigrasday.com), and the week leading up to it, the entire city is just one big party. The date varies from year to year, but it always falls 46 days before Easter.

MARCH. The **Tennessee Williams New Orleans Literary Festival** (☎ 504/581-1144; www.tennesseewilliams.net) features readings, theater performances, workshops, and more in honor of Williams, an honorary New Orleanean. On **St. Patrick's Day** (www.stpatricksdayneworleans.com), the city celebrates its Irish heritage (yes, it has a significant one) with three parades and (surprise!) some drinking.

APRIL. The **French Quarter Festival** (☎ 504/522-5730; www.fqfi.org) is a huge free fest featuring local food and music on the streets and parks of the Quarter. During the two weekends of Jazz Fest, the

New Orleans Jazz & Heritage Festival (☎ 504/410-4100; www. nojazzfest.com), the New Orleans Fair Grounds transforms into 12 stages of music featuring everything from blues to pop to R & B by little local bands and top artists. Add killer food and cool art to equal massive good times.

MAY. Over 75 restaurants, 150 national vintners, and 10,000 people participate in 4 indulgent days of tastings, dinners, and seminars, and a huge strolling street party at the **New Orleans Wine & Food Experience** (NOWFE; ☎ 504/934-1474; www.nowfe.com).

JULY. The **Essence Music Festival** (☎ 504/523-5652; www.essence. com/festival) is a major, 3-day event celebrating African-American culture with music and self-improvement workshops.

SEPTEMBER. At **Southern Decadence** (☎ 504/522-8047; www. southerndecadence.net), parading, dancing, costuming, and all manner of over-the-top outrageousness are the hallmarks of this LGBTQ celebration.

OCTOBER. On Halloween weekend, the **Voodoo Music & Arts Experience** (www.voodoofestival.com) brings alternative rock and costumed attendees to City Park for this major 3-day event.

NOVEMBER-DECEMBER. The **Celebration in the Oaks** (☎ 504/483-9415; www.celebrationintheoaks. com) is a festival of lights set among the giant oaks that can be viewed on foot, by car, or by miniature-train ride. During **Christmas New Orleans Style** (☎ 504/410-2396; http://holiday.neworleans online.com), the city becomes even more magical with riverside bonfires, light shows, concerts, home tours, Reveillon dinners, and community caroling.

Useful Websites

- *Times-Picayune* (newspaper): **www.nola.com**
- *New Orleans Advocate* (newspaper): **www.theneworleans advocate.com**
- *Gambit* (local alt-weekly): **www. bestofneworleans.com**
- *Offbeat* (monthly entertainment guide): **www.offbeat.com**
- *Ambush Magazine* (LGBTQ magazine): **www.ambushmag. com**
- WWOZ-FM (local radio station with nightclub listings): **www. wwoz.org/livewire**

Also recommended, the following apps:

- RTA's **GoMobile** (for bus and streetcar info and passes), **Parking Panda,** and **Parkmobile**
- **Uber, Lyft,** and if you're in town for Mardi Gras, WWL-TV's **Parade Tracker**
- All major events in town will have worthwhile apps as well.

Cell Phones

In general, it's a good bet that your U.S. phone will work in New Orleans, though service can be spotty in some hotels, especially those that were converted from old, thick, brick-walled warehouses.

However, foreign visitors' service varies (as do rates). Assume nothing—call your wireless provider and get the full scoop. Or, pick up a cheapie pre-paid cell phone to use for the duration of your visit. **Walgreens** has them (☎ 504/568-1271; 900 Canal St.).

Car Rental

If you plan to hang out in the French Quarter or Central Business

District (CBD), you're better off walking or using cabs. Parking is expensive and hard to find. If you truly need a rental car, all the major rental companies operate in the city. For the best rates, shop well in advance and avoid picking up and dropping off at the airport. The **Parkmobile** and **Parking Panda** apps are very useful.

Getting **There**

By Plane
If you fly into New Orleans, you arrive at the mid-sized **Louis Armstrong International Airport (MSY),** about 25 minutes outside the city. The much smaller **Lakeshore Airport** has service for private planes and a few regional commercial flights.

Getting into Town from the Airport by Cab
A taxi ride to the French Quarter or CBD from the airport will cost you $36 for one or two people and an additional $15 each for three or more people. There are cab stands outside the baggage claim areas at both ends of the airport. **Uber** picks up in the Ground Transportation Center (GTC), the structure across the street.

All cab companies take credit cards. Tipping 10 to 15% is standard (Uber includes tip costs in its fare.)

Getting into Town from the Airport by Van or Bus
Airport Shuttle (☎ 866/596-2699) ferries visitors from the airport into city hotels for $22 one way. The vans make multiple stops, but it's cheaper for single travelers. Purchase tickets at kiosks in the baggage claim area (or in advance at www.airportshuttleneworleans.com). Wheelchair accessible shuttles are available by advance arrangement.

Jefferson Transit public bus #E-2 departs from the upper level of the airport and goes as far as Tulane Avenue and Loyola Street in the CBD—a 30- to 40-minute ride. One-way fare is $2. From there riders can transfer **to other lines on the New Orleans Regional Transit Authority** (NORTA) lines (additional $1.25 fare). More info for Jefferson Transit Authority at ☎ 504/818-1077; www.jeffersontransit.org; for NORTA at ☎ 504/248-3900 or www.norta.com. Also see below about the Jazzy Pass.

By Car
If you drive to New Orleans, you'll take one of the major thoroughfares: the Pontchartrain Expressway (Hwy.) 90 or Interstate 10.

The former is best if you're heading to the Garden District or Warehouse District; the latter if your destination is Uptown or the French Quarter.

By Train
Your train will arrive at the **Union Passenger Terminal,** 1001 Loyola Ave. (☎ 800/USA-RAIL or 504/528-1610; www.amtrak.com) in the CBD, just a few blocks from the French Quarter. (Interesting side note: The station temporarily served as a post-Katrina jail.) Taxis are readily available outside.

Getting **Around**

On Foot
The city is flat, which makes it perfect for walking and wheelchairs if the weather cooperates. Do be wary of uneven sidewalks, though, as there are plenty.

By Public Transportation
Visit www.norta.com or call the **Regional Transit Authority's Ride Line** at ☎ 504/248-3900 for maps, passes, and other information about streetcars or buses. Any of New Orleans's visitor information centers (including the main location at 529 St. Ann St. by Jackson Square) also have information on public transportation.

Buses connect most New Orleans neighborhoods, though depending on your destination, you'd do best to take the more scenic streetcar when possible. Transfers cost 25¢, and buses are wheelchair accessible.

Fares on public buses and streetcars are $1.25 each way, exact change is required. Alternately, the **Jazzy Pass** is a fantastic deal if you plan to use public transportation frequently. It's available at **Walgreens** drugstores and machines at major streetcar stops; the downloadable **GoMobile** app lets you carry the pass on your smartphone. Passes include 1-day ($3), 3-day ($9), or 31-day ($55) passes and are good on all buses and streetcars.

By Streetcar
Since 1835, the **St. Charles streetcar line** has serviced the CBD, the Garden District, Uptown, and Carrollton, 24 hours a day. The **Canal streetcar line** is a 5½-mile (8.9km) ride up Canal through the CBD and Mid-City, and ends at one of two destinations: either north on the Carrollton spur to City Park (p 82) or farther west to the Cypress Grove and Greenwood cemeteries. The **Riverfront streetcar line** runs along the riverfront from the Convention Center to the French Quarter at Esplanade Avenue. The **Loyola line** runs along Loyola Avenue from the Greyhound and Amtrak stations to Canal Street. All streetcars except the historic St. Charles line are wheelchair accessible.

By Taxi or Rideshare
After dark, cabs and rideshares are recommended. Except during the busiest events and rush hours, they're plentiful and easy to find in the French Quarter and CBD (but call ahead for a taxi if you're in a rush). **Uber** or **Lyft** cars are usually only a few minutes away, and are a good option (unless you're travelling across town or to the airport during surge pricing, in which case taxis are still a better deal). Rates are $3.50 for the initial charge, plus $2 per mile (25¢ per ⅛ mile) thereafter. Add $1 for each additional person. The maximum number of passengers is five. Most cabs take credit cards, but ask before your driver starts the meter. **United Cab** (☎ 504/524-9606; www.unitedcabs.com) is the largest and most well-utilized; **Metry Cab** is also good (☎ 504/835-4242; www.metrycab.com).

By Bike
The city is flat and relatively compound, making bikes a great option for those who are comfortable riding city streets. **Bicycle Michael's** (☎ 504/945-9505; www.bicyclemichaels.com) and **American Bicycle Rentals** (☎ 504/324-8257; www.bikerentalneworleans.com) are two good bets for rentals. For

maps, bicycling events and related resources, visit **www.bikeeasy.org**.

By Car

To drive in New Orleans is to be masochistic. Parking is a pain, finding your way is tough because the city's streets follow the twists and turns of the river, and local drivers often make last-minute lane changes and exits. Avoid it if at all possible.

Fast **Facts**

AREA CODE The area code for the greater New Orleans metropolitan area is **504.** The North Shore, the region north of the city across Lake Pontchartrain, which includes Slidell, Covington, and Mandeville, is **985.**

ATMS ATM machines using the global networks **Cirrus** (☎ 800/424-7787; www.mastercard.com) and **PLUS** (☎ 800/843-7587; www.visa.com) are all over the city—including all hotels and most bars. You shouldn't have trouble finding one, but most impose a fee for use ranging from $1 to $5. Most but not all establishments take credit cards, so it's wise to carry some cash. But not a lot. Always use caution when obtaining cash.

BABYSITTERS Ask your hotel or call one of the following agencies for sitting services: **Accents on Children's Arrangements** (☎ 800/539-1227; www.accentoca.com), or **Dependable Kid Care** (☎ 504/486-5044; www.dependablecare.net).

BUSINESS HOURS On the whole, most shops and stores are open from 10am to 6pm. Banks open at 9am and close between 3 and 5pm.

CONVENTION CENTER The **Ernest M. Morial Convention Center,** 900 Convention Center Blvd. (☎ 504/582-3000; www.mccno.com), sits at the end of the Warehouse District, on the river between Thalia and Water streets; the Riverfront streetcar drops you off at the Convention Center.

DENTISTS Contact the **New Orleans Dental Association** (☎ 504/834-6449; www.nodental.org) to find a recommended dentist near you.

DOCTORS For urgent care, we've had good experiences at **New Orleans Urgent Care,** 900 Magazine St. (www.neworleansurgentcare.com; ☎ 504/552-2433), or in the French Quarter at 201 Decatur St. (☎ 504/609-3833).

EMBASSIES & CONSULATES All embassies are located in the nation's capital, Washington, D.C. Some consulates are in major U.S. cities, and most nations have a mission to the United Nations in New York City. For addresses and phone numbers of embassies in Washington, D.C., call ☎ 202/555-1212 or log on to www.embassy.org/embassies.

EMERGENCIES For fire, police, and ambulance call ☎ 911. For the **Poison Control Center,** call ☎ 800/222-1222. The **Travelers Aid Society** (1615 Canal St., Suite B; ☎ 504/412-3700; www.tasnola.org) renders emergency aid to travelers in need. If a hurricane threatens, ask your hotel concierge to help you arrange for transportation out of the city.

GAY & LESBIAN TRAVELERS New Orleans has an extensive and active LGBTQ community. For resources, start with **Ambush Magazine,** 828-A Bourbon St. Ambush Magazine (☎ 504/522-8049; www.ambushmag.com). **Faubourg Marigny Art and Books (FAB)** (600 Frenchmen St.; ☎ 504/947-3700) also serves as an unofficial info source.

HOLIDAYS Banks, government offices, and post offices are closed on the following legal national holidays: January 1 (New Year's Day), the third Monday in January (Martin Luther King, Jr. Day), the third Monday in February (Presidents Day), the last Monday in May (Memorial Day), July 4 (Independence Day), the first Monday in September (Labor Day), the second Monday in October (Columbus Day), November 11 (Veterans Day), the fourth Thursday in November (Thanksgiving Day), and December 25 (Christmas). Also, the Tuesday following the first Monday in November is Election Day and is a federal government holiday in presidential-election years (held every 4 years). Stores, museums, and restaurants are open most holidays, except for Thanksgiving, Christmas, and New Year's Day.

    Note: Mardi Gras day is considered a holiday in the greater New Orleans area, and most businesses are closed or have shortened hours.

HOSPITALS For emergency care, call 911 or go to the emergency rooms at **University Medical Center** (2000 Canal St.; ☎ 504/702-3000; www.umcno.org) and **Tulane University Medical Center** (1415 Tulane Ave.; ☎ 504/988-5263; www.tulanehealthcare.com/er).

HOT LINES Louisiana Rape Crisis is ☎ 800/656-4673; **Travelers Aid Society** is ☎ 504/586-0010; **Gamblers Anonymous** is ☎ 504/431-7867; **Narcotics Anonymous** is ☎ 504/899-6262; **Alcoholics Anonymous** is ☎ 504/838-3399.

INSURANCE The best way to find an insurance policy is to go to one of two marketplace websites: InsureMyTrip.com and Square-Mouth.com. Each will lead you to respected companies, and show you the wide range of policies available for your trip.

LIQUOR LAWS The legal drinking age in New Orleans is 21, and despite the city's easy-going reputation, bars and liquor stores do check for proper I.D. and police make arrests for illegal behavior. You can buy liquor most anywhere 24 hours a day, 7 days a week, 365 days a year. All drinks carried on the street must be in plastic cups; most bars provide complimentary plastic "go-cups" so that you can transfer your drink as you leave. Many a vacation has been ruined by trouble or arrest for drunk and disorderly or driving while intoxicated arrests. Know your limits; assign a designate; don't be a statistic.

LOST & FOUND Be sure to notify all your credit card companies the minute you discover your wallet has been lost or stolen, and file a report at the nearest police precinct (☎ 311). Your insurance company may require a police report before covering any claims. Many credit card companies can wire you a cash advance immediately or deliver an emergency credit card in a day or two. **Visa's** U.S. emergency number is ☎ 800/847-2911 or 410/581-9994. **American Express:** ☎ 800/221-7282. **MasterCard:** ☎ 800/307-7309 or 636/722-7111. You can also have money wired to you via **Western Union** (☎ 800/325-6000; www.westernunion.com).

    If you lost something at the airport, call **Airport Operations** (☎ 504/464-2671 or -2672). If you lost something at a security checkpoint, call the **Support Operations**

Center at ☎ 504/463-2252. If you lost something on the bus, call ☎ 504/940-5586, or on the street-car, call ☎ 504/827-8399. If you lost something anywhere else, phone the **New Orleans Police nonemergency line** (☎ 504/821-2222). You may also want to fill out a police report for insurance purposes.

MAIL The main post office is at 701 Loyola Ave. In the French Quarter, there is one at 1022 Iberville St.

NEWSPAPERS & MAGAZINES To find out what's going on around town, pick up a copy of the *Times-Picayune* (www.nola.com) or *Gambit* (www.bestofneworleans.com). *OffBeat* (www.offbeat.com) is a comprehensive monthly guide to the city's evening entertainment, art galleries, and special events; it's available in most hotels.

PARKING In the French Quarter, you're better off in a pricey parking lot rather than risk parking in an illegal spot. If you park on a parade route or block someone's driveway, your car will be towed to the **impounding lot** (☎ 504/565-7235) or the **Claiborne Auto Pound,** 400 N. Claiborne Ave. (☎ 504/565-7450). Prepare to pay a hefty fine of $100 or more.

PASSPORTS Visitors from foreign countries must have a passport to enter the United States. Always keep a photocopy of your passport with you when traveling. If it's lost or stolen, having a copy facilitates the reissuing process at a local consulate or embassy. Keep your passport and other valuables in either the hotel's or the room's safe.

PHARMACIES The **Walgreens** at 1801 St. Charles Ave. (☎ 504/561-8458) is the closest one to the French Quarter that offers 24-hour pharmacy service.

POLICE For nonemergency situations, call ☎ 504/821-2222. For emergencies, dial ☎ 911.

RESTROOMS Public restrooms are located at Jax Brewery, Riverwalk Marketplace, Canal Place Shopping Center, the French Market, and major hotels.

SAFETY New Orleans's neighborhoods can change from block to block—good areas can turn to unsafe ones in a matter of moments. Always be aware of your surroundings and change course as your spidey sense indicates. Women should consider substituting a backpack for your usual purse or simply don't carry one. Public transportation is fine during the day but a cab is best at night. Stick to the main tourist areas and travel in pairs or groups. Don't flash your cash or your new iPhone. Keep your wits about you; don't look for trouble (or drugs, or any other illegal activity), and generally make smart decisions like your mama taught you.

TAXES In general, the total sales tax in New Orleans is 9% (9.75% in the French Quarter; 13% for hotel rooms plus a $.50 to $3 per night).

TELEPHONES For directory assistance ("information"), dial ☎ 411. Hotel surcharges on long-distance and local calls are astronomical, so you're usually better off using a cellphone. Public pay phones are hard to find nowadays.

TIME ZONE New Orleans is in the Central Standard Time (CST) zone. Daylight saving time is in effect from the second Sunday in March through the first Sunday in November.

TIPPING In hotels, tip bellhops at least $1 per bag and tip the chamber staff $1 to $2 per day (more if you've left a disaster area); the same for the doorman or concierge if he or she has provided you with some specific service. Tip valet-parking attendants $1 to $2 when they get your car. In restaurants, bars, and nightclubs, service staff and bartenders expect 15 to 20% of the check, and checkroom attendants $1 per garment. Tip cab drivers 15% (at least $2), skycaps at least $1 per bag, and hairdressers and barbers 15 to 20%.

TRAVELERS WITH DISABILITIES
Organizations that offer resources and assistance to travelers with disabilities include **MossRehab** (☎ 800/CALL-MOSS; www.moss resourcenet.org), the **American Foundation for the Blind** (AFB; ☎ 800/232-5463; www.afb.org), and **SATH** (Society for Accessible Travel & Hospitality; ☎ 212/447-7284; www.sath.org). **AirAmbulanceCard.com** is now partnered

with SATH and allows you to preselect top-notch hospitals in case of an emergency. **Access-Able Travel Source** (☎ 303/232-2979; www.access-able.com) offers a comprehensive database on travel agents from around the world with experience in accessible travel.

Flying Wheels Travel (☎ 507/451-5005; www.flying wheelstravel.com) and **Accessible Journeys** (☎ 800/846-4537 or 610/521-0339; www.disabilitytravel.com) are two of the many travel agencies specializing in travelers with disabilities.

In the U.K., contact **Holiday Care** (☎ 0845-124-9971; www.tourismforall.org.uk).

New Orleans: **A Brief History**

1682 French explorer René-Robert Cavelier, Sieur de LaSalle, claims the land near the mouth of the Mississippi and dubs it Louisiana in honor of King Louis XIV.

1718 New Orleans is founded as a valuable port city by Pierre Le Moyne, Sieur d'Iberville, and named in honor of Philippe, Duc d'Orléans.

1762–1800 After Louis XIV gave Louisiana to his Spanish cousin, King Charles III, the French Quarter burned down twice, which explains the Spanish influence on architecture.

1794 Pioneering farmer Etienne de Boré invents a way to extract sugar from cane, which remains a boon crop to this day.

1800 Louisiana is returned to the French.

1803 Napoleon secretly sells the Louisiana territory to the United

States, best known today as the Louisiana Purchase.

1805 The city of New Orleans officially incorporates.

1812 Louisiana becomes the 18th state of the United States of America.

1815 Battle of New Orleans is a pivotal moment in defeating the British for good in the War of 1812.

1832–33 More than 10,000 citizens die during the horrific yellow fever and cholera epidemics.

1837 Mardi Gras is reported on for the first time by the press.

1840 Now in its heyday, New Orleans is the fourth-largest city in the country and the second-largest port city after New York. Antoine Alciatore founds Antoine's Restaurant, initiating city's foodie repute.

Mardi Gras Lingo

Talking the talk and walking the walk are crucial if you plan to go to New Orleans during Mardi Gras. Here's how to sound like a native:

- **Ball or Tableau Ball:** Krewes host these themed, masked balls. Themes change from year to year.
- **Boeuf Gras:** The fatted calf, which represents ritual sacrifice, as well as the last meal eaten before Lent, the Roman-Catholic season of fasting leading up to Easter. It's also the symbol of Mardi Gras and the first float of the Rex parade.
- **Carnival:** A pre-Lenten celebration beginning January 6 (the 12th night after Christmas) and ending Mardi Gras day.
- **Court:** A krewe's king, queen, and attendants.
- **Doubloon:** Collectible toy coins thrown by krewes during parades. They feature the logo of the krewe on one side and its theme for a particular year on the other.
- **Fat Tuesday:** Otherwise known as Mardi Gras, the last day before Ash Wednesday, which is the first day of Lent.
- **Favor:** Krewe members give these souvenirs, which feature the krewe's logo and date, to people who attend their ball.
- **Flambeaux:** Flaming torches carried by parade marchers, traditionally African-Americans.
- **King Cake:** A ring-shaped, sugared pastry decorated with purple, green, and gold (Mardi Gras colors) that contains a small doll representing the infant Jesus.
- **Krewe:** The traditional word for a Carnival organization.
- **Lagniappe** (pronounced *lan*-yap): Loosely means "a little extra," and refers to any small gift or token, even a scrap of food or a free drink.
- **Lundi Gras:** The Monday before "Fat Tuesday." New Orleaneans celebrate with a mini festival and concert along the Mississippi. Late in the day, the Mayor presides over a ceremonial meeting of the Kings of the Rex and Zulu krewes, which officially starts Mardi Gras.
- **Mardi Gras:** French for "Fat Tuesday." Technically, if you say "Mardi Gras day," you're really saying "Fat Tuesday day."
- **Rex:** Latin for "king." The King of Carnival is Rex.
- **Second line:** A group of people that follows a parade, dancing to the music. Also, a musical term that specifies a particular shuffling tempo popularized in much of New Orleans music.
- **Throw me somethin', mistah!:** The traditional bead-seeking call. (Note: displaying nude body parts in exchange for beads is neither required nor legal.)
- **Throws:** Inexpensive trinkets, toys, and symbolic knickknacks tossed. The most coveted throws are the gilded coconuts of the Zulu Social Aid and Pleasure Club and glittery shoes thrown by the ladies of the Muses krewe.

1850 The rampant slave trade, fueled by the cotton industry, makes New Orleans the largest slave market in the nation.

1862 New Orleans is captured by Union soldiers.

1865–77 Time of Reconstruction, when carpetbaggers come in droves and change the city's social and economic dynamic.

1890 Arrested for boarding the "wrong" train, Homer Plessy decides to sue the state, paving the way for the landmark segregation legislation *Plessy v. Ferguson*.

1892 The St. Charles streetcar goes electric.

1900 Birth of Louis Armstrong, iconic musician, actor, and informal ambassador of all things New Orleans.

1911 First use of ".Jazz" when Razzy Dazzy Spasm Band performs in New York, and another band co-opts its name as Razzy Dazzy Jazzy Band.

1928 Radical populist Huey P. "Kingfish" Long becomes governor of Louisiana, then later a member of the U.S. Senate.

1935 Long is shot at the Louisiana Capitol in Baton Rouge and dies 2 days later at the age of 42.

1938 Playwright Tennessee Williams moves to the Crescent City.

1956 Lake Pontchartrain Causeway, the world's longest bridge, is completed.

1960 Integration of public schools.

1964 The original Canal streetcar is replaced with buses, which are hit with tomatoes by protesting locals.

1975 Louisiana Superdome opens with great fanfare and mixed reaction.

1977 Ernest N. "Dutch" Morial becomes the city's first African-American mayor.

1984 Redevelopment inspired by the Louisiana World Expo helps the local economy during the dramatic '80s oil bust.

2000 The National World War II Museum opens.

2004 The Canal streetcar reopens with air-conditioned, handicapped-accessible red cars.

2005 Multiple levees break during Hurricane Katrina, destroying a large portion of New Orleans and killing 1,833 people throughout the southern U.S.

2010 British Petroleum's oil rig *Deepwater Horizon* explodes and sinks, killing 11 workers and discharging 4.9 million barrels of oil into the Gulf of Mexico. "Who Dat" frenzy ensues when underdog Saints win first Super Bowl championship in team's 43-year history. HBO's *Tremé* TV series debuts.

2018 City of New Orleans' 300th anniversary.

Index

See also Accommodations and Restaurant indexes, below.

Photo **Credits**

cover left, Dustie / Shutterstock.com; cover middle, Courtesy of Commander's Palace; cover right, photosounds / Shutterstock.com; p ii, top, © Cheryl Gerber Photography; p ii, second, GTS Productions / Shutterstock.com; p ii, third, Fotoluminate LLC / Shutterstock.com; p ii, fourth, Courtesy of Muse; p ii, last, © Cheryl Gerber Photography; p iii, top, Courtesy of Commander's Palace; p iii, second, © Cheryl Gerber Photography; p iii, third, Austin Kirk; p iii, fourth, Courtesy of Ace Hotel/ Fran Parente; p iii, last, © Cheryl Gerber Photography; p viii, Britt Reints; p 1, Britt Reints; p 4, top, Jeff Turner; p 4, bottom, © Cheryl Gerber Photography; p 5, top, Robbie Mendelson; p 5, bottom, © Cheryl Gerber Photography; p 6, top, © Cheryl Gerber Photography; p 6, bottom, Robbie Mendelson; p 7, © Cheryl Gerber Photography; p 9, giblcho; p 9, bottom, Lawrence Roberg; p 10, Ryan Lackey; p 11, © Cheryl Gerber Photography; p 13, top, Dan Merino; p 13, bottom, Fotoluminate LLC / Shutterstock.com; p 14, Infrogmation of New Orleans; p 15, top, Steven Depolo; p 15, bottom, Infrogmation of New Orleans; p 17, top, © Cheryl Gerber Photography; p 17, bottom, © Cheryl Gerber Photography; p 18, © Cheryl Gerber Photography; p 19, GTS Productions / Shutterstock.com; p 21, David Berkowitz; p 22, © Cheryl Gerber Photography; p 23, top, Michael Homan; p 23, bottom, Loco Steve; p 25, Kimberly Vardeman; p 26, © Cheryl Gerber Photography; p 27, Teemu008; p 29, © Cheryl Gerber Photography; p 30, © Cheryl Gerber Photography; p 31, © Cheryl Gerber Photography; p 33, Joseph Sohm / Shutterstock.com; p 34, © Cheryl Gerber Photography; p 35, Infrogmation of New Orleans; p 37, top, © Cheryl Gerber Photography; p 37, bottom, © Cheryl Gerber Photography; p 38, top, © Cheryl Gerber Photography; p 38, bottom, T. Tseng; p 39, Infrogmation of New Orleans; p 41, top, Jon Lebkowsky; p 41, bottom, Malcom Manners; p 42, top, nola.agent; p 42, bottom, PunkToad; p 43, Fotoluminate LLC / Shutterstock.com; p 45, top, © Cheryl Gerber Photography; p 45, bottom, Louisiana Travel; p 46, © Cheryl Gerber Photography; p 49, top, David Ohmer; p 49, bottom, David Ohmer;p 50, © Cheryl Gerber Photography; p 53, © Cheryl Gerber Photography; p 54, top, Chris Waits, p 54, bottom, David Ohmer; p 55, bottom, Michael McCarthy; p 55, top, © Cheryl Gerber Photography; p 57, © Cheryl Gerber Photography; p 58 top, © Cheryl Gerber Photography; p 58 bottom, © Cheryl Gerber Photography; p 59, Infrogmation of New Orleans; p 61, Infrogmation of New Orleans; p 62, Infrogmation of New Orleans; p 63, Larry Johnson; p 65, © Cheryl Gerber Photography; p 66, top, Infrogmation of New Orleans; p 66, bottom, Robbie Mendelson; p 67, Hrag Vartanian; p 69, top, amadeustx / Shutterstock.com; p 69, bottom, © Cheryl Gerber Photography; p 70, Infrogmation of New Orleans; p 71, Courtesy of Muse, p 76, Courtesy of Hove; p 77, Courtesy of Fleur de Paris; p 78, top, Courtesy of Meyer The Hatter; p 78, bottom, Courtesy of Sucre/ Kaela Rodehorst Photography; p 79, Courtesy of New Orleans Glassworks & Printmaking Studio; p 80, © Cheryl Gerber Photography; p 81, © Cheryl Gerber Photography; p 83, © Cheryl Gerber Photography; p 84, © Cheryl Gerber Photography; p 87, top, © Cheryl Gerber Photography; p 87, bottom, Louisiana Travel; p 88, © Cheryl Gerber Photography; p 91, top, Louisiana Travel; p 91, bottom, © Cheryl Gerber Photography; p 92, Louisiana Travel; p 93, Courtesy of Commander's Palace; p 99, © Cheryl Gerber Photography; p 101, top, Courtesy of Compere Lapin; p 101, bottom, © Cheryl Gerber Photography; p 102, top, Infrogmation of New Orleans; p 102, bottom, Courtesy of Emeril's; p 103, top, Courtesy of Galatoire's; p 103, bottom, Courtesy of Gautreau's/ CHRIS GRANGER; p 104, top, Infrogmation of New Orleans; p 104, bottom, Courtesy of Herbsaint/ Chris Granger; p 105, top, © Cheryl Gerber Photography; p 105, bottom, Courtesy of Ace Hotel/ Fran Parente; p 106, Besh Restaurant Group/ Graham Blackall; p 107, top, Courtesy of R'evolution; p 107, bottom, Courtesy of Shaya/ Randy Schmidt; p 109, © Cheryl Gerber Photography; p 110, Dion Hinchcliffe; p 117, top, Jessep; p 117, bottom, © Cheryl Gerber Photography; p 118, © Cheryl Gerber Photography; p 120, © Cheryl Gerber Photography; p 121, top, © Cheryl Gerber Photography; p 121, bottom,© Cheryl Gerber Photography; p 122, top, © Cheryl Gerber Photography; p 122, bottom, Louisiana Travel; p 123, Austin Kirk; p 124, © Cheryl Gerber Photography; p 128, © Cheryl Gerber Photography; p 129, Tom Pumphret; p 130, top, Tom Pumphret; p 130, bottom, © Cheryl Gerber Photography; p 131, top, © Cheryl Gerber Photography; p 131, bottom, Noah Kern; p 133, Courtesy of Ace Hotel/ Fran Parente; p 134, Courtesy of Grand Victorian Bed & Breakfast; p 139, Courtesy of Ashton's Bed & Breakfast; p 141, Courtesy of The Chimes Bed & Breakfast/ Victoria Pisarello; p 142, top, © Cheryl Gerber Photography; p 142, bottom, © Cheryl Gerber Photography;p 143, Courtesy of Lowes New Orleans; p 144, top, Courtesy of Old No. 77 Hotel & Chandlery; p 144, bottom, © Cheryl Gerber Photography; p 145,

Map **List**

Notes

Notes

Notes

Notes